difficult . . . and then seeing all of the pieces fall miraculously into place. *Finding Zoe* is a joy to watch unfold."

—Jill Smokler, *New York Times* **bestselling author**
of *Confessions of a Scary Mommy* **and**
Motherhood Comes Naturally (And Other Vicious Lies)

"A must-read for any adoptive parent, or anyone considering adoption. Brandi Rarus's story of *Finding Zoe* is an amazing reminder that the power of love overcomes life's most challenging obstacles and nothing can stand in the way of what's meant to be."

—**Mary Donahue, Senior Vice President of Non-Fiction**
at Lifetime Television Network, and adoptive parent

"Just as my character on *Switched at Birth* has helped to expose the Deaf community for what it really is to our mainstream TV audience, so too does *Finding Zoe* break down the barriers between the hearing and Deaf communities by showing Deaf Culture in ways never seen before . . . deaf people and deaf families with identity issues and conflicts universal in scope . . . seeking the love that all of us need . . . and the compelling lessons learned by being human. Bravo to *Finding Zoe*."

—**Sean Berdy, actor on the ABC TV hit series,**
Switched at Birth, **and Peabody Award Recipient**

"*Finding Zoe* shines an unbiased light on teen pregnancy, adoption, and the sacrifice parents make to find the best home for their children. A must-read for teenagers and

their parents, or for anyone else who may be contemplating their choices for an unintended pregnancy."
—Jan and Bob Charnecki,
founders of Options Pregnancy Center

"A work of both heart and mind, driven by the authors' passions to describe our rich history as deaf people, that paved the way for deaf children like Zoe . . . a book that both deaf and hearing people have longed for."
—Greg Hlibok, student leader of the
Deaf President Now protest at Gallaudet University

"This isn't just a book for people interested in adoption; it's an inspiring story that will touch the heart of anyone with a connection to children and families—which is to say, almost everyone."
—Adam Pertman, Executive Director of Donaldson
Adoption Institute, and author of *Adoption Nation*

"This really hits home . . . The story of a deaf baby who finds her way to a deaf family . . . and embraces her culture and language. A great introduction to the Deaf community."
—Chris Wagner, President
of National Association of the Deaf

A DEAF WOMAN'S STORY OF IDENTITY, LOVE, AND ADOPTION

Finding Zoe

Brandi Rarus
AND Gail Harris

BENBELLA BOOKS, INC.
DALLAS, TEXAS

BenBella Books, Inc.
10300 N. Central Expressway
Suite #530
Dallas, TX 75231
www.benbellabooks.com
Send feedback to feedback@benbellabooks.com

Printed in the United States of America
10 9 8 7 6 5 4 3 2 1

Library of Congress Cataloging-in-Publication Data
Rarus, Brandi.
Finding Zoe: a deaf woman's story of identity, love, and adoption / by Brandi Rarus and Gail Harris.
pages cm
Includes bibliographical references and index.
ISBN 978-1-940363-22-6 (hardback)—ISBN 978-1-940363-45-5 (electronic)
1. Rarus, Zoe. 2. Rarus, Brandi. 3. Deaf women—United States—Biography.
4. Deaf children—United States. 5. Deafness—United States. 6. Adoption—United States. I. Harris, Gail. II. Title.
HV2534.R37A3 2014
362.4'2092—dc23
[B]
2014014707

Editing by Erin Kelley
Copyediting by Julie McNamee
Proofreading by Amy Zarkos and Cape Cod Compositors, Inc.
Cover design by Connie Gabbert
Text design by John Reinhardt Book Design
Text composition by Integra Software Services Pvt. Ltd.
Printed by Lake Book Manufacturing

Distributed by Perseus Distribution
perseusdistribution.com

To place orders through Perseus Distribution:
Tel: 800-343-4499
Fax: 800-351-5073
E-mail: orderentry@perseusbooks.com

Significant discounts for bulk sales are available. Please contact Glenn Yeffeth at glenn@benbellabooks.com or 214-750-3628.

For Edgar Bloom—
for your dedication to activism and paving the way
for deaf people today

For Jess and BJ—
for giving me the gift of Zoe

For my sons, Blake, Chase, and Austin, without whom my
journey to Self would not be complete. I love you more than
life itself. **B. R.**

For Bill and Lucas—
Thank you for bringing yourselves to me every day.

For George Jaidar, my teacher—
I live to see through your eyes. **G. H.**

CONTENTS

Foreword   XIII

Preface   XVII

PART I

My Winding Road

	Prologue	3
CHAPTER ONE	Suddenly Soundless	5
CHAPTER TWO	Changed by a Deaf Priest	26
CHAPTER THREE	Deaf President Now	43
CHAPTER FOUR	Full Circle	69
CHAPTER FIVE	Our Family Hears	94

PART II
The Roads of Others

CHAPTER SIX   Jess and BJ   111

CHAPTER SEVEN   Love's Sacrifice   137

CHAPTER EIGHT   The Right Thing to Do   175

PART III
The Roads Converge

CHAPTER NINE   Providence Provides   195

CHAPTER TEN   Waiting All Our Lives   213

Epilogue   233

Acknowledgments   255

About the Authors   263

Resources   265

FOREWORD

ALL CHILDREN COME into our lives for a reason. Some are born to us, some are the children of friends or family, and some are brought to us through miracles. Some miracles come easy; others are disguised by struggles and weighted with challenges and tough decisions. *Finding Zoe* is the story of remarkable connections that entwined four families and led one baby girl away from perceived limitations and into the home of the mother—and family—that was meant to raise her.

I met Brandi Rarus for the first time when she became my understudy in the play *Children of a Lesser God* at the Immediate Theatre Company in Chicago. As teens, the two of us grew up in different suburbs of Chicago, but we shared the common experience of navigating our way through the mainstream at rival high schools. Midway through the play's run, I captured the part of Sarah Norman in the movie version of *Children of a Lesser God,* and, at the age of 21, I became the youngest recipient of an Academy Award.

My work has honored me with the privilege of world-wide travel, where I have met deaf and hard-of-hearing children from all walks of life. Like Brandi, I have always moved easily between the hearing and Deaf communi-ties, but rather than seeing the separation between the two, I recognize that we all live in one world—a world in which our differences can be celebrated. I learned long ago to embrace who I am and what I believe in, and Brandi experiences a similar journey in *Finding Zoe*.

Since those early days, our lives have taken off in different directions, but our paths continue to cross at various events within our Deaf community. Like Brandi, I'm a mother of four children, a role that has always kept me centered and grounded in the midst of a whirlwind acting career. I know without question that the love a mother has for her child is fierce and strong and that whether that child is biological or adopted, a mother's heart knows no boundaries. Zoe began her life with two extremely young parents, a first set of adoptive parents, and foster parents, and then found her way into the hearts of Brandi's family—where she belonged all along. *Finding Zoe* isn't just the story of a deaf child's journey; it is a story of love, heartache, sacrifice, and celebration.

Our stories in life are never really about what divides us anyway. Instead, they are about what brings us together in love, in sacrifice, in our heartaches, and in our joys. They are about how we survive when hope fades and how we rise above the crush of our own self-doubt. What we discover along the way is that our own perceptions are critical to our happiness and that our miracles are always found in acceptance and celebration of our differences.

—MARLEE MATLIN, ACADEMY AWARD–WINNING ACTOR

PREFACE

OW FITTING THAT Brandi would ask us to write the preface for this beautiful, telling story. Not only was Alan the director of the National Technical Institute for the Deaf (when Brandi was a bubbly, young student there in the late 1980s) and is now the president of Gallaudet University—both of which have given us a connection to her for many years—but also, in so many ways, our backgrounds and experiences as parents are similar to hers and her husband Tim's.

We can appreciate what a lucky child Zoe really is. To have parents like Brandi and Tim who are so involved in our Deaf community has given Zoe the opportunity to continuously learn about her culture—that of being deaf and proud. It didn't surprise us when a few years back, Brandi uprooted the entire family, moving them from Clearwater, Florida, to Austin, Texas, just so that Zoe could attend the Texas School for the Deaf.

As is evident from reading this tale, Brandi was meant to be Zoe's mother. We were in awe of Brandi's life story and are grateful to her for baring her soul and writing personally and candidly about her experiences. As president of Gallaudet University, Alan is proud to be a part of the "Deaf President Now" legacy, shared so intimately and meaningfully in this book—the first we'd ever read that covers this monumental movement in Deaf History from such a personal perspective.

The story is sure to inspire both deaf and hearing people alike about things concerning adoption, being true to yourself, holding on to your dreams, and turning your life around. Perhaps from reading this book, another deaf couple will be blessed with adopting a deaf child someday.

The truth is, every child—deaf and hearing—should be blessed with a family as loving and as in tune as Zoe's (including her three older hearing brothers), and as this book is passed on throughout our community, some three million strong, for generations to come, we're sure that it will help that vision to manifest.

—T. ALAN HURWITZ AND VICKI T. HURWITZ,
President and First Lady, Gallaudet University

". . . Zoe, the Greek word for life as God has it."

—MAX LUCADO, *3:16: THE NUMBERS OF HOPE*

PART I

My Winding Road

PROLOGUE

Z OE SAT CROSS-LEGGED on the living room floor, her
palms cupping her chin, her mouth agape. "Do it
again, Daddy!" she said. "Do it again." Tim's hands
flew as he painted a landscape of Santa with his sleigh and
reindeer, zooming across the starlit sky, then landing on the
roof and squeezing down the chimney. Snow was falling,
and the moon was dark. With his hands and facial expressions, in American Sign Language (ASL), Tim was creating
a magnificent vista, telling the story of the fat man getting
stuck in the chimney . . . and Zoe was laughing.

It was 2006 and the Christmas I had always dreamed
about having but thought might never happen. My eyes
drank in my two-and-a-half-year-old daughter, *my daughter,*
in a Christmas storybook scene, her sparkling eyes revealing her deep sense of peace and belonging. That afternoon
was my own private miracle. Watching Zoe filled me with
such joy, I could hardly contain it. For a second, I worried
again that, just maybe, I loved her *too* much—and that my
three sons felt that I loved them less. This is my cross. No

matter how many times they tell me how much they feel my love, I can't help feeling that way.

It has to do with the fact that Zoe, like me, is deaf.

Within my community, the Deaf community, my situation is somewhat rare because most deaf people have never also been hearing. It's been a gift of sorts as it allows me to be with hearing people one minute and deaf people the next, and generally, to be at ease around hearing people. Because I could already speak before I became deaf, I do have some speech—what I call a "deaf voice." At first, most people think that I sound funny, but after a short while, they are usually able to understand me. Because I lip-read, I never give a second thought to going into Starbucks and asking for a cup of coffee. I know what to expect: I'm going to ask for the coffee; they're going to ask me if I want room for cream. I'll say yes; they'll tell me how much it costs. I'll pay and then leave. I feel in control of the situation.

This ease with life was not easily won; however, it was inextricably linked to my desire for a daughter, something I'd been aware of ever since I was a little girl. When each of my three sons was born, each was my pride and joy. Yet their births just widened the hole that could only be filled by my having a daughter, for a reason I had yet to discover. As I look back on my life, with the gift of time and hindsight revealing everything, it was as if God had swooped down from above and said, "Here's your *deaf* daughter. You, Brandi, of all people, deserve her."

The first step of that journey began one fateful day in March of 1974.

Chapter One

SUDDENLY SOUNDLESS

THE BLINDING LIGHT is what I remember most. I wanted to put my hands over my eyes but was too weak to do so. It was 2:00 AM, and I was lying face up in the emergency room, more scared than I can say. I don't remember much else before being electrocuted, or so it felt, but I do remember the doctor turning me over, pushing aside my hospital gown, and rubbing my lower back with alcohol. I can smell it now.

Then came the blow—a sharp prick sending excruciating shock waves up to my head and down to my toes. I let out a scream, which my mother, who was outside in the hallway, couldn't bear to hear. I was only six years old. The doctor had given me a spinal tap, and there was nothing left for my mother to do except swallow her tears and wait for the results.

Thus began two weeks of hell for her and two weeks of drifting in and out of sleep—rather peacefully—for me. The days leading up to that night, when I was burning up with a fever, had been much worse for me. I remember reaching into the freezer for ice cubes to put on my forehead. It was March 1974; I was in kindergarten. We lived in Naperville, Illinois, a suburb of Chicago. My mother had already taken me to the doctor, who said that I had a bad flu but I would be okay. He was so wrong.

The day she took me to the hospital, I had been lying on the living room couch. My mother had come over and sat down next to me. "How's my sweetie?" she asked. I shook my head. She kissed me on the forehead and then went into the kitchen to talk to my father. "Bill, call the babysitter to cancel," she said. "We can't go out tonight." They had theater tickets for a show that was playing in Chicago. My mother came back to me and took me upstairs to my room. I must have fallen asleep because I remember waking up, hours later, and feeling like I was going to die. I called my mother. She came running into my room. "Mom, I don't feel good," I told her.

"Can you put your chin to your chest?"

"It hurts," I told her, after trying. She couldn't remember how she knew to ask that question, but remembered that if the answer was no, it was a very bad sign. I was wearing my favorite pink-and-white pajamas, and she picked me up, wrapped me in a blanket, and then took me to the hospital while my father stayed home with my brother, Bryan, who was a year and a half younger than me. The doctor who admitted me said that it looked like I had spinal meningitis, but that the spinal tap would confirm his diagnosis.

About an hour after my mother heard me scream, the doctor came into the waiting room to talk to her. "Mrs. Sculthorpe, please sit down." My mother's heart skipped a beat. "It is spinal meningitis—a very bad case. We're doing everything we can, but you need to be prepared. We're not sure if she'll make it through the night."

That's when my mother turned to the doctor and said, "She will not die, doctor. She will not die." Years later, those words would make me stronger.

They put me in isolation and gave my mother a gown and mask to put on before coming to my room. A profoundly spiritual woman, that night she felt betrayed by God. *Where are you?* she asked him silently. *Why is this happening? Why are you letting this happen?* She sat in my room and wept for hours, holding my hand.

The night passed. I didn't die. Then the next passed. When it started to look as if I were going to live, the question then became what havoc the illness would wreak upon my body. Deafness, epilepsy, blindness, or any combination of the three were all possibilities, the doctors said. My parents were just relieved that I wasn't going to die.

But the horror continued.

For fifteen days, I drifted in and out of sleep, the little veins in my arms collapsing from the IVs, so they had to put them between my toes and in my feet, with my mother still asking God, *Why?*

Finally, one sunny morning, I awakened. My father came over and sat on my bed and started talking to me. He was telling me about all of the people who had said hello, saying, "Heather and Heidi [my twin cousins], Grandma, Aunt Linda, Uncle Jerry, Doris . . ." I understood him until he got to my cousin Doris, and then I asked, "Who?" He thought that I didn't remember who Doris was, but that wasn't it at all—I didn't recognize the shapes his mouth was forming. At that moment, I experienced a strange sensation of silence and knew that something wasn't right. It's my most vivid memory from that time because it was when I first realized that I could not hear. Finally, when I understood "Doris," we moved on.

From that moment on, lipreading became my way of "listening" to people. The adjustment happened so quickly, seamlessly, and matter-of-factly that I don't even remember missing hearing people's voices—or at least, I didn't allow myself to. I don't think that I was lipreading right off the bat, yet I don't remember struggling with the sudden loss of communication. The inclination to lip-read just took over. Knowing what I do now, I believe that I was in a readied state. It was as if I had been given the talent to lip-read.

Nevertheless, at the time, it was all so confusing. I had been so sick, and this new silence was so strange that I didn't understand what had happened to me. Looking back, I think that my strong need to survive, to get back to the life I knew as fast as I could, had already kicked in with full force, and I didn't even fully grasp that I could no longer hear.

My parents, however, were beginning to grasp it. Once or twice, my father talked to me with his back facing toward me, and, of course, I didn't answer, which keyed him right into what the doctors had said. Then there was the day when he and my mother had arrived at my hospital room around noon, and we spent the afternoon sitting around talking (I got as much of the conversation as I could), watching TV, playing cards, and reading magazines. I also napped for a while and was quickly regaining my strength. Late in the afternoon, one of the window shades in the room suddenly flipped up, making a loud noise—*pfpfpf-pfpfpf-pfpfpf*. I didn't stir. My mother, already hypervigilant to my impending symptoms, really became concerned.

An hour later, when the pediatrician came to check on me, she told him how I hadn't reacted to the loud noise. He put his watch to my ear and asked me what I heard. "Tick tock," I told him.

"She can hear," he said.

I don't remember if I actually heard the sound of the watch, or if I just *thought* I did—if my brain "heard" the sound because it knew that's what it was supposed to do. It's a phenomenon called *phantasmal hearing,* and it happened again.

I remained at the hospital for another week and then went home. In spite of everything, I wasn't scared or upset in the hospital or when I came home—just confused because of all the enormous changes.

For example, I quickly learned to rely on vibrations. Whenever my mother was cooking in the kitchen and needed me, she stomped her foot on the floor. I felt it sitting at the kitchen table and looked up, knowing that she wanted to tell me something. Then there were the lights. Whenever I was upstairs in my bedroom and she or my father needed me to come downstairs, they flicked the lights on and off at the bottom of the stairs. I saw the lights flickering in the downstairs hallway and knew to come down. We all quickly adjusted that way.

In spite of all the changes, I don't think there ever was a particular moment in time when it hit me, "Oh my God, I'm deaf," and I never talked about it with my parents— or anyone, for that matter—which seems a bit odd to me now. My mother told me, though, that about a month after I had come home from the hospital, she found me sitting on my bedroom floor with my records and record player just watching a record spinning around and around and around. Such stories make me think that if there wasn't an exact moment in time when I realized I was deaf, it was because I *didn't want there to be.*

When I finally did come to the realization that I was deaf—that I couldn't hear anything—I was mad at my mother, at first, for never having told me that there was such a thing as *deafness*. What a shock. Not that I was deaf, but that there actually were *people who couldn't hear.* I had heard of blind people or of people in wheelchairs, but not deaf people.

Still, after being home from the hospital for just a few days, I was ready for the entire ordeal to be over. I wanted to play with my toys and my friends. I was a child, resilient, living in the moment. I could communicate, read, and write. I wanted go to the pool. I wanted to have fun. My mother thinks that I pretended half the time because I didn't want her to be upset. But I swear that was not how I experienced it.

During the first few months, she took me to doctors and audiologists in Chicago, thinking that someone would tell her that my hearing would come back and that I'd be okay. But no one did. I remember her dragging me to all those doctor appointments, but I thought that I was just going to get my "ears checked" and was bored to tears. I wanted to be playing outside with my friends instead of sitting there with microphones on my head waiting to raise my hand when I heard something—which I never did. The sounds would get so loud that I felt the vibrations on the earphones or my eardrums would pop. Then I would raise my hand, but I wasn't actually hearing sounds, just feeling vibrations.

They gave me hearing aids, which never helped. Yet I wore them all through elementary school. In the hearing-impaired classroom, the teacher used a microphone to amplify the sound of her voice. Everyone thought that the hearing aids might help me to hear *something*. My mother also wanted me to wear them because it let the hearing kids know that I was deaf.

At first, I wore a body hearing aid, which was supposed to be more powerful than the over-the-ear kind. The little doohickey sat in a small, white cotton pouch that was strapped to the middle of my chest. Straps went under my arms and over my shoulders, connecting in the back like a bathing suit. From the front, two wires went up to my ears.

I wore the pouch over my clothing because it always needed adjusting. I remember eating chicken soup a lot and the soup dripping onto the hearing aids and soiling the straps. Later, I wore the pouch under my clothes. I wore it for three years and then switched to an over-the-ear hearing aid, which I lost at O'Hare Airport when someone walked off with my little pocketbook.

Eventually, my mother mourned my hearing loss and everything that came with it, which I believe was so

ME AT SIX YEARS OLD WITH HEARING AIDS

incredibly healthy. However, at first, she worried about how I'd ever survive in the world as a deaf person. She wanted me to be like I was before. She wanted to be able to talk to me and for me to be able to *hear* her. Turning inward, she asked God to help her to say and do the right things for me; praying pulled her through. Yet she questioned if she believed enough and had enough faith, hoping that if she prayed hard enough, I would get better.

At the same time, she was very angry at God because I had become deaf—that he had allowed it to happen. She couldn't understand why she had experienced so much support from family and friends—that God had been there for her, but not for me.

As a child, had I known how she had suffered over this, I would have told her straight out that I'd never doubted for even a second that God had been with me. And now, as I sit here writing this book, with Zoe asleep in the next room, I know it even more. Years later, my mother would meet deaf adults who were happy and successful and raising families of their own just like hearing people, and it would help her realize that I was going to be just fine. The professionals had told her right from the start that I had a natural talent for lipreading and that not everyone does. This made her feel hopeful. After about a year, she finally accepted that I was deaf; both she and my father took sign language classes and supported me in more ways than I ever could have asked for.

One of my fondest memories is sitting with her in the living room and watching *Little House on the Prairie*.

She interpreted for me in sign language. She sat on the fireplace hearth, and I sat on the floor. That was in third grade. Later, in eighth grade, while she was getting my brother and me off to school every morning before rushing off to work herself, my girlfriends would call to say what they were wearing, which really slowed us down, but she always put up with it and told me, wanting me to feel like I was one of the crowd.

It was different with my dad. He's less emotional than my mother and more or less deals with things as they come. Of course, he was very saddened that I had lost my hearing, even a bit angry at first as well. It was hard for him to have a hearing daughter one day and deaf the next. I think he was comforted though by how well I seemed to be adjusting. He was proud of me for that. Later he would say that had I been another child, he might have worried more, but that my self-confidence made *him* confident that things would work out and that I handled everything better than anyone possibly could have. He was also comforted and felt rewarded by the fact that my close friends in the neighborhood just accepted me for who I was and were still my friends. That's what really let him know that everything was going to be all right.

One of my favorite memories with my dad is going to these father/daughter events called Indian Princesses. Grasping sign language hadn't come all that easy for him, which I think he may have felt a little bad about, but I remember him interpreting for me at those gatherings. He was Big Feather, and I was Little Feather. I also remember him occasionally taking me to the mall to go clothes shopping. He was never overprotective or anything when we did things together. After a while, for both my parents and for me, my being deaf just became the way it was.

My close friends were very supportive from the start by just being regular with me, which truly meant the world to me. The fact that I was an extremely self-confident child helped me to adjust as well. The only difficulty I had was feeling dizzy the first few weeks after coming home from the hospital, due to an imbalance in my ears. I remember having to crawl around the front yard; it was a bit slanted and was easy for me lose my footing.

At times, I thought I was getting my hearing back—I'd swear that I'd heard something, like the church organ when we went on Sundays and the sound of the waves at the beach when we visited my family in New Jersey. I would hear them crashing inside my head. But it was more phantasmal hearing; ultimately, I always faced the silence. Today I can still remember the sound of that church organ, and the waves crashing, and the sound of paper crumbling, though they grow more and more distant. I have no memory of voices.

The fall after I became deaf, I started first grade in a school that had a deaf program. To maintain my speech, my mother wanted me mainstreamed in a regular classroom with hearing children. I had a resource teacher who worked with me one-on-one. I was the only deaf student in the entire class. I watched the deaf kids in the class next door and copied what they did. Years later, my mother told me that I pretended to sign, using signs that had no meaning, like a child playing make-believe. I also fiddled with my hearing aid wires and the controls. Eventually, it became clear that I needed more support; so in second grade, I finally went into a deaf class and loved it.

It was an "oral" class, meaning that the teacher spoke and didn't use sign language. We read her lips, so I continued using my speech, as my mother had wanted (as do most hearing parents who have a deaf child). I had already grasped the essentials of English: pronunciation, syntax, inflexion, even idioms, which had all come by ear. I had the basis of a vocabulary, which would only be enhanced by reading, and I continued reading at home with my parents. There were only three students in the class—Tom Halik and Tommy Miller, who could both hear a bit and had spoken language, and *completely deaf* me. Every day, I'd watch our teacher, Mrs. Kutz—with her long black hair cut in a feathered, wispy style and her huge smile—write on the overhead projector (this allowed us to absorb things by having the benefit of a visual aid) and read her lips all day long.

It was then that I became more aware that I was different. In first grade, I had done pretty much whatever the other kids did, but with the work becoming more academic, I began realizing that I was missing directions and puzzled about some of the assignments. Mrs. Kutz discovered that I couldn't spell well and began giving me additional help.

The class next door to mine was for the deaf kids who used sign language and didn't use their voices at all; they were students who were born deaf or who had lost their hearing prelingually (the more common scenario compared to mine).

Those were the kids who taught me how to sign.

I had started picking it up from them from the moment I'd started school—at recess, in gym, and while sitting with them on the school bus day after day after day. By the end of first grade, I was signing right along with them.

In fourth grade, I finally made my first deaf girlfriend, Lisa, and it was a big deal to me. Other than the kids at school, I played with my hearing friends from the neighborhood. Even though Lisa and I spoke in class, we signed when we played together. I remember the day my father drove me to Lisa's house for the first time my mother was just overjoyed.

It's amazing to me now when I remember that when Lisa and I played together, we couldn't watch television or go to the movies. (Today, it's hard to imagine Zoe *not* in front of the TV.) But closed-captioning wasn't available then; it didn't become widely available until the early 1990s. Lisa and I couldn't even listen to music. But life was good.

There were challenges. Once, I was left in the stacks of the school library during a fire drill. There were childhood trials. Even though my closest friends remained true, other kids teased me. The kids in the playground made fun of the way I talked. (Not being able to hear my own voice impacted my speech.) Once, a kid asked me if my hearing aids went through my head. "Yeah, right through my braaain," I told him, thinking what a jerk he was. Some kids didn't even believe I was deaf, so I took them to my house to show them the "Caution, Deaf Child" sign that my mother had put on the front lawn.

I hated that sign with a vengeance. "Why do I need a sign to tell cars about me?" I wanted to know. My mother just wanted them to slow down, of course. What I hated most was riding in the bus for "special needs" kids, which the year before my friends and I had named the "baby" bus. It was half the size of the regular bus. Other people may have thought I was different, but to me, I was still the same. I wasn't handicapped or special, and I certainly didn't need a sign or a baby bus. I didn't want to be different, and I didn't want to be labeled. Yet, even though I was unable to express those concerns, I was more upset by them than by the fact that I was deaf.

In third grade, we got a new swim coach. Even though none of my previous swim coaches had ever coached a deaf kid before, this coach was so closed-minded and was very uncomfortable around me; he honestly believed that my being deaf limited my swimming ability. He took me out of the lineup, which really angered and humiliated me because I had never been behind with my start: I would wait for the smoke to appear from the starting gun when it went off, and then, bam, I was off. I was one of the best backstroke swimmers and had been on the swim team every summer. It was the first time that anyone had made me feel like a second-class citizen because I was deaf. Fortunately, my mother spoke to the coach, he put me back in the lineup, and things worked out after that.

Despite the few mishaps, I *had* adjusted very well to being deaf. I was succeeding academically, I had become a good lip-reader and signer, and I still had speech. Even though a few kids in the playground wouldn't play with me anymore, I was thriving socially; when my deaf friends weren't at my house playing, my hearing friends were. I was part of the crowd and having fun, doing homework, and joining in after-school activities. My desire to do well, be accepted, and please others, such as my parents and teachers, especially since becoming deaf, also helped—as did my self-confidence.

Who knows whether that confidence came from an intense drive to do my best or from my connection with God and knowing that I'd be taken care of. One way or another, I've just always been that way. We went to an Episcopal church at the time (later, after my parents divorced, we switched to a Lutheran one), but it was my own individual connection to God that nurtured me and allowed me to become strong. Somehow, I always wanted to be better than average and to do something first class with my life. Becoming deaf might have traumatized another child, but not me; I think that it has made me a better person. It has forced me to raise the bar in everything I do and has helped me to become more self-aware, giving me the opportunity to go beyond my comfort level, be less prejudiced, and relate well to people who are "different."

Facing such a huge loss at a young age forced me to see how people treat one another and what it's like to grow up in America as part of a minority. The experience also gave me a different perspective on living with the majority—being deaf in a hearing world. My world was silent. I was cut off from communicating and had to learn to survive through that.

The world operates through spoken language. I had to think ahead, be more aware, be more alert, and take on challenges I might not otherwise have taken on. Today, I can't listen to the radio as I drive to work in the morning; hear announcements over a PA system; or, if it isn't captioned, watch TV. Often, because of communication barriers, I have to work twice as hard as a hearing person. Instead of it taking me five minutes to make a doctor's appointment, it takes me ten.

At home, I use a videophone to make phone calls. When I am talking with a deaf person, I see them signing to me on a screen. It's sort of like Skyping; we just sign back and forth to each other. To connect with people who don't have a videophone, I use something called Video Relay Service. So when making a doctor's appointment, for example, I sign to a video relay interpreter I see on my screen, who then interprets what I said for the nurse on a telephone.

It takes extra time. First, I have to make sure that the interpreter is voicing for me correctly so that the nurse is getting the correct information, which I do by reading their lips. Then, I have to request that an interpreter is present at the appointment, and if the nurse isn't familiar with the Americans with Disabilities Act (ADA), I have to educate her that this is my right. It's like that for deaf people in the mainstream. By now, of course, living that way has become second nature. I don't even think about it.

Back then, I started compensating without thinking much about it either. It was funny. When I first became deaf, people started treating me differently, although I still felt like I was just like everyone else. But as time passed, the reverse happened. My family and friends in the neighborhood told me that despite my being deaf, I functioned just fine, that it seemed as though I were hearing, and that I was bright and could make it in the hearing world. They said that I didn't need to be with deaf people at all. Yet, even though I inherently knew that what they were saying was wrong, that being deaf *did* make me different, even with all my confidence—I tried so hard to convince myself that what they were saying was true. I really took what they said to heart.

While I had some deaf friends at school, at home, I usually socialized with the hearing kids in my neighborhood and was the only deaf kid in the whole group. One of my best friends was a girl named Chris D'Alessandro, who lived down the block from me. Even though Chris was a year older than I was and was a grade ahead of me in school, we hung out after school and on the weekends. She quickly learned how to sign and became my advocate and champion. Chris made sure that I was included in all the conversations with our gang, and she called my mother on the phone to coordinate our plans for me. I was more grateful to her than I could say.

When I entered junior high, even though I was main-streamed in a public school that had a deaf program, I chose not to participate in the deaf classes most of the time. I took regular classes and had a sign-language inter-preter with me throughout the day.

I thought I was too smart for the deaf classes.

I didn't know that deaf kids who are only exposed to sign language and don't use any speech whatsoever—like the kids in the class next door to me in elementary school—often read below grade level because their English isn't honed. Mistakenly, I associated reading below grade level as being less intelligent. Most of those kids didn't speak either, which I also mistook as a sign of being less smart. I sure was wrong.

In eighth grade, the pull to prove to myself and every-one else that I could "stay hearing" was stronger than ever. I left the deaf program altogether and transferred to my neighborhood junior high school, which was right up the street and where all of my hearing friends went. I didn't want to be in a "special" school anymore. I wanted to walk to school with my friends and be a part of it all. I was the only deaf student in the entire school, and they gave me a full-time interpreter named Joyce Zimmerman. Joyce sat near my desk in every class and interpreted for me. She was awesome because she blended in, giving me space when I needed it, but was always there when I needed her. She would meet me at each class but did not follow me there. She let me be independent and did not come to recess or lunch.

That year, I became president of the student council. When I first ran for office, I read my speech over the intercom and then had a friend reread it to be sure that everyone understood. Once elected, I used my voice to run meetings and do other things; Joyce would sign to me what people said. In ninth grade, I remained local as well, attending Naperville Central High School with my neighborhood friends and, again, was the only deaf student in the school.

That was the year when things really began changing for me.

Central High had so many more students and teachers than my previous schools, none of whom knew me or my family. Despite having my friends there, who were as welcoming as usual, and Joyce, who interpreted for me all throughout high school, I began feeling very isolated. My self-inflicted pressure to stay hearing still remained in full force and began taking its toll on me. Chris still had very high expectations of me, and because she was older than me, I looked up to her. She really believed I could be successful in the mainstream and continued to support my success. I would hear her voice in my head saying, "You're *not* different; you can do it!" I didn't want to let her down or let myself down. I was proud of myself for being able to manage in that hearing world and in a hearing high school, and that pride felt good.

It was the era of *Flashdance*, and, believe me, I knew what was "in" with those hearing girls. Chris made sure of that. We went to see *Rocky* when it first came out, and she taught me the popular song from the movie, "The Eye of the Tiger." She would tap the beat on my leg, and I mouthed the words. In the same way, my hearing friends taught me all the popular songs of the time: "Last Dance," "Hard to Say I'm Sorry," "Time for Me to Fly." I so appreciated them for teaching me those songs because it made me feel like I was part of the group.

But life was a mixed bag. I was missing things. At the Lutheran Church, I didn't have an interpreter, so during my confirmation classes, I had no idea what was going on when they read from the Bible. I just sat there, wondering what was happening in the silence. Later on, my interpreter from school, Joyce, joined my church, so I got lucky.

Once during summer vacation, I went to the movies with my twin cousins, Heather and Heidi. They were identical twins, beautiful girls with dark brown hair. They were my age, and we had grown up together. To them, I was just Brandi, their cousin, not Brandi, the deaf girl. I had gone to the movies a few times with my father—who was an avid James Bond fan. The movies were heavy-duty action and easy to follow, so I was looking forward to going with my cousins. Heather and Heidi were the most fun people for me to hang around with—always daring and getting into trouble. We fed each other popcorn and had sodas. We had gone to see the Chevy Chase movie *National Lampoon's Vacation* (which wasn't closed-captioned, of course).

Perhaps it was because of the amount of dialogue, but I didn't understand a thing. *What's so funny?* I thought. As I watched my cousins laugh, while I sat there in silence, I was painfully reminded that my hearing was not what it was supposed to be. I was beginning to feel very different and alone.

The thing about lipreading is this: even though I'm very good at it, at best I can only follow 50 percent of what's going on, which is usually enough for me to get the gist of the conversation and respond appropriately, but sometimes it isn't. One-on-one, I communicated very well. I did fine. But in a group, it became impossible to lip-read what everybody was saying. At night, it really became difficult when I couldn't see my friends' faces. Yet, I thought about my deaf friends, over there in the deaf program, whom I saw on the weekends and at other times, playing around and having fun with deaf people whom I hadn't met yet, and I started longing to be a part of that.

I was caught between two realities, yearning for fuller communication and to be around deaf people, yet feeling that gigantic pull toward the hearing world; my friends' and family's influence on me was just so huge. I knew that they were all well intentioned when they told me that I was fine in the hearing world. But deep inside, I began feeling more and more that I *was* different and functioned differently than they did, and that they were so wrong.

Chapter Two

CHANGED BY A DEAF PRIEST

THE SPRING OF 1984, toward the end of my freshman year, was brutal. Torn between wanting to stay in the hearing world and yearning for a fuller connection with deaf people, I realized I needed to decide whether to stay at Central High or transfer the following fall to Hinsdale South, which had a deaf program and was thirty minutes from my home. When I mentioned it to Chris, she was extremely disappointed that I would even consider Hinsdale South. She just genuinely believed that Central was the best place for me and that I could make it there.

I agonized over the decision for weeks; no one knew what I was going through, not even my mother. I couldn't express it, but at fifteen years old, I knew that I wasn't just choosing a school—I was choosing a life. Staying at Central meant I'd probably go to a college such as Illinois

State with my friends, marry hearing, and remain in *that* world. Going to Hinsdale South meant I'd probably go to Gallaudet University or National Technical Institute for the Deaf (NTID), marry a deaf person, and be in the Deaf World. Being on the fence—dabbling in both worlds but never fully embracing either—no longer felt tolerable.

It was an overwhelming decision, yet my heart knew the answer—and had known it all along. I finally chose Hinsdale South and that year said good-bye to my hearing friends from the neighborhood. I couldn't articulate to them why I was leaving; I just told them that I was going to South, to the deaf program. I didn't know how to say that I felt tired and defeated from playing a game I knew I couldn't win and wasn't good for me anyway. How could I tell them that I was mourning the life I had known since I was six, or that the things I had done had been fun and had served me well but could no longer lead me where I needed to go? On some level, I think they understood. After that, I only saw them when we bumped into one another on the street, and it was always bittersweet.

I'd made my decision in the spring but avoided telling Chris until school was almost out. I was too scared to tell her, for fear of disappointing her. Carrying that pressure around inside me all that time felt awful. I think she knew I was avoiding her. I remember the day I finally told her very well. I went to her house, and, through my tears, told her that I was leaving Central. She ended up being more upset that I had *been so scared to tell her.* She said that it was okay, that what was important was that I had "tried."

I walked home feeling so much lighter. I knew then that I was really done with that part of my life—and I wasn't looking back.

I had no regrets, but it was tough. Half of it was that I thought I would miss my friends and that I was disappointing them, which was devastating. But the other half, which I was finally acknowledging, was that I felt like *they* had disappointed *me* by telling me I was someone I wasn't, by saying that I could function as a hearing person, and by making me feel that I wasn't meeting their standards. I was very hard on myself, striving to stand tall, and yet I felt as if I had failed in their eyes.

I prayed to find peace with my decision, find acceptance and peace with myself. I needed peace with my life, my family, my neighborhood friends, and the world. Although I didn't agree with everyone's claim that I was normal like them, I wasn't savvy enough to explain to them how I felt or what I needed. I wasn't able to say that even though I walked down the hallways in school with a big smile on my face, a deep-down part of me wanted to curl up in the corner and have everybody leave me alone. I remember walking over to the cornfields about a block from my house one day and just sitting there, in the middle of the stalks, trying to come to terms with it all. I was longing to hear some wisdom that would help me see the light. I didn't want to feel like the lone soldier out there.

I arrived at Hinsdale South and loved it. The school had 2,000 hearing students and 150 deaf students—so many more than in elementary school and junior high, as the deaf kids from each district came to Hinsdale. They all took classes in the deaf wing—except me. Even after making the huge decision to switch schools, I still avoided the deaf program and took all my core classes with the hearing kids, with the use of a sign language interpreter. Part of me still believed that I was smarter than the other deaf students, and I still needed to cling to what was familiar and to what I thought people expected of me. I was still entrenched in the hearing world and was not ready to loosen the ties.

Even so, I took a few classes with the deaf kids, like Health and Consumer Education, and these classes ended up being my favorites. I just loved the direct communication and soaked it in; it was so much more fulfilling than finding out what was going on through an interpreter. I socialized with the deaf kids at lunch, in gym class, and after school, as well, becoming part of a group and the culture I craved.

The summer between my sophomore and junior years, twenty of us went to a deaf camp in the Adirondack Mountains in Upstate New York; we all took the bus there together. This Catholic camp, called Camp Mark Seven, was run by a deaf priest named Father Tom. I had no expectations—my friends were going, so I went along. We arrived right before dinnertime and checked into our dorms.

Whoa. I had walked into a different world, into Deaf Culture, and into the Deaf community.

Everyone there was either deaf or they signed—the counselors, cooks, maintenance people, lifeguards—right down to the nurse. It wasn't participating in the camp

activities with my deaf friends that made the difference—
I'd done lots of activities with them at school—the difference was that the entire staff was also deaf. Until that time,
I had never really interacted with a single deaf adult. These
days, it's different; but back in the 1980s, most teachers
for the deaf, like those at South, were hearing. My parents and relatives were all hearing. In the Deaf Culture,
we talk about the 90 percent rule: 90 percent of deaf parents have hearing children, and 90 percent of deaf children have hearing parents. Over the years, I've met deaf
children who thought they were going to die by the time
they reached eighteen because they had never met a deaf
adult. Many certainly don't believe they can make it in the
general culture.

It was as if I could finally believe in my future.

For the first time since I was six years old, I was signing
with deaf adults in an environment where communication
was 100 percent accessible to me. I had *full* communication. No more missing out on parts of conversations; no
more feeling like I wasn't being understood. For two whole
weeks, I was smack in the middle of everything and soaked
it up like nothing before—helping out in the mess hall and
making meals with George the cook, and helping the life-
guard put away the pool chairs. When I rode home on the
bus two weeks later, I immediately felt like my communication was gone—like the air was just being sucked out of me.

My camp counselor, Carla, was a psychology major at
Gallaudet College (later called Gallaudet University). She
had an air of confidence about her—she was independent

and had dreams of her own; having that camper-counselor relationship with her allowed me to see beyond Naperville and Hinsdale South and realize that there was a life out there waiting for me. Even though we rarely talked specifically about being deaf, I never forgot the time we did because her words have become my mantra for raising Zoe. We were sitting by the archery court one afternoon.

"You think much about being deaf?" I asked.

"You mean how it impacts your life and stuff?"

"Yeah," I said.

"Not really," Carla said. "I learned long ago that you need to make it your friend—you won't get through life if you don't."

"Hmm . . . never thought about it that way."

"Yeah, Brandi," she said. "Whatever you do, you have to embrace that you are deaf, but don't *ever* let it define you."

The camp was called Mark Seven because in the Bible, Mark 7 references Jesus healing a deaf person. I remember Father Tom telling us those particular verses—verses 7:31, 34, and 35. All of the campers were sitting down by the lake with the tall trees surrounding its circumference and providing shade, where every morning he gave his daily sermons and workshops; the outdoors was our chapel.

"Jesus heals a deaf man," he signed, his round-rimmed glasses reflecting the sunlight. "Looking up to heaven, he sighed and said, *Ephphatha*, which means, 'Be opened.' Instantly the man could hear perfectly, and his tongue was freed so he could speak plainly." He continued, "*Ephphatha* means empathy—be thou open. When Jesus said it to the deaf man, it meant, 'open your ears and you become hearing.'"

A chill went up my spine. Immediately, I understood, "Be thou open," to mean: be open to life, to people, to ideas; be accepting. Don't judge. Already I knew that I was more open and accepting of others than most—like a mother figure—although I was too young then to realize that it was because of having experienced my own loss, of having become deaf. By fifth grade, I was able to discern what people were really thinking, yet not judge them. Even though I hadn't walked in their shoes, I could understand them and what they were about. I'd made fun of the kids who were riding the "baby" bus one year, and the next, I was riding it myself. Although I couldn't articulate these thoughts back then, on some level, I grasped that people's differences added richness and soul to life and to being human. Hearing Father Tom's words that day helped me to understand that a little bit better.

Late one afternoon, Father Tom was talking to us down by the water, his straight, dark brown hair looking jet black, with the sun hiding behind the trees. He had a medium build and was wearing black pants and a paisley green shirt.

"How many of you are proud to be deaf?" he asked, in his kind and unassuming manner.

No one raised their hand. I remember thinking, *This man is crazy.*

He continued on, "It was a difficult job for God to make people because he had to give each person a completely different personality and appearance." He thought for a second and then continued signing. "So, to make it easier for himself, he made one recipe for the human body."

I sat there, listening intently.

"Yet, he made a different body recipe, a special one, for deaf people. God put more effort into making this unique group of people," he said. "Being deaf is a gift from God."

Wham. Bam. I felt like I had been punched in the stomach.

It wasn't that I heard him say to me that being deaf is a gift from God, but that *being deaf is okay*—not only okay but something good, if I let it be!

Nobody had ever said that to me before. Oh, I'm sure that my parents, friends, and teachers wanted me to generally feel good about myself. But Father Tom's words validated my very existence as a deaf person. They were a lifeline connecting me to *Me*, helping me to see that I wasn't crazy for feeling different, that I felt different because, good God, I *was* different, and nothing that anybody could say would ever again make me believe otherwise.

My new awareness was shaky, like a foal first standing on its legs, but that afternoon a window had opened, and I saw that being deaf was the way I was *meant to be*. At that moment, I knew that going back to Central High for that first year had been a wasted year; I had been trying to prove to everyone that I was hearing, instead of knowing that being deaf was okay.

I realized that I had a choice: I could continue trying to be "hearing" (having hearing friends and taking hearing classes) and fail, or I could be the best deaf person I could be. It was then that I began seeing my being deaf through the eyes of self-acceptance and understanding that it didn't mean I was failing.

After returning home from camp, I got a job at the Colonial Ice Cream Shop. I worked fountain and just loved eating the ice cream and making all those sundaes. The "Turtle" was made from two pumps of hot fudge, one pump of caramel, and pecans over vanilla ice cream. Another popular sundae, the "E.T.," named after the movie released that summer, was made from one pump of peanut butter, two pumps of hot fudge, and Reese's Pieces over vanilla ice cream.

It was at the Colonial that I fell for a hearing guy, and fell hard, beginning a love affair that ultimately led me to discover my deep capacity to give and to receive love. My very first day on the job, Matt came right over to me and said, "Hey gorgeous," and I thought, *Hey gorgeous, yourself.*

Matt was seventeen; he was tall with dark brown, curly hair and green eyes and was as kind as he was versatile. He not only worked fountain with me but also did just about every other job in the joint—host, cook, waiter, supervisor. He was different from the crowd: steady, responsible, and loved having a good time. As soon as we began hanging around together, he learned to finger spell (signing words, letter by letter). Then, he bought *The Joy of Signing*, a popular book back then, and studied signing with a vengeance, picking it up quickly, which I really appreciated.

Occasionally, it was Matt's job to lock up the shop at night after everyone had gone home. I'd hang around, so it was just the two of us there all alone at midnight. He'd whip up a couple of Monte Cristos or patty melts, and we'd sit at a booth and eat. I brought my great-grandmother's sterling silver candlesticks from home, which we hid in the ceiling right above the booth and took down whenever we dined.

But Matt's love notes were what I appreciated most of all; they made me fall in love with him. Every night around midnight, when I wasn't at the restaurant with him, he'd drive by my house on the way home from work and leave me a letter in my mailbox. Some were strictly love letters; others were his thoughts about his day and other musings; we couldn't communicate by phone, so letter writing took its place. First thing every morning, I ran to the mailbox to get his note, and then I'd write back, leaving my note in the mailbox in the afternoon for him to pick up that evening. Rather than receiving phone calls from my boyfriend, like hearing girls did, I received his amazing love letters. For once, being deaf had its privileges, and it was my secret—receiving little treasures that the hearing girls would never know . . . a whole box full of them. Matt had a way with words that went straight to the heart.

Summer turned to fall, and once school started, my life was very full. Besides spending time with Matt, my horizons expanded in the deaf circles when I played the role of Lydia in the Chicago stage production of *Children of a Lesser God* and became Marlee Matlin's understudy. Lydia wasn't the lead role; she was one of the students at the school for the deaf. The Immediate Theater Company—an off-Broadway-caliber company—had been looking for

ME AND MATT AT MY SENIOR PROM

someone to play the role and saw me perform it in our high school's performance of the show, which they came to scout. (Throughout the years, I had participated in "Deaf Drama" as an extracurricular school activity.) The company offered me the role without even auditioning. However, my mother made me turn it down because she thought that it would place too big of a burden on my school schedule. But she agreed to let me be Marlee Matlin's understudy.

When the show ran that summer, Marlee was in the middle of callbacks for the movie for the lead role of Sarah and was gone quite a bit, so I got to perform several times. Back then I did it just for fun. However, I can see now how acting on stage before hundreds of people in the role of a deaf character was a step toward later being on stage before thousands of people representing deafness for real.

From the outside, my life was good; I had a fun job, a great boyfriend, and tons of friends, and I was performing—but on the inside, it was altogether different. Camp had begun my journey toward self-acceptance, but by being with Matt all the time, working at the Colonial, living with my hearing family, and still taking the hearing classes at school, I remained that hearing girl at heart, while my struggles continued to grow.

At Matt's graduation party at his parents' home, he was busy entertaining and couldn't be with me very much, and I felt uncomfortable in the crowd. The same thing occurred at his grandmother's Thanksgiving dinner: I felt so out of place at that table. Even working at the Colonial—something that I had enjoyed immensely— became more difficult for me to handle. Yes, one-on-one my lipreading was good, but the Colonial was a busy place; usually there were too many conversations happening at once. And just because I could easily talk to a single individual does *not* mean that people would take the time to talk to me; and when they did, it was usually to give me instructions, not make social talk. That is a big difference. Feeling increasingly left out of the social scene and more and more isolated, having Matt around was my saving grace.

When it came time to choose a college, I went where my deaf friends were going: the National Technical Institute for the Deaf (NTID), which is part of the Rochester Institute of Technology (RIT) and is located in Upstate New York. NTID attracted deaf students like me who came from hearing families, had been mainstreamed in public school, and were "oral."

My other option, Gallaudet University, which is located in Washington, DC, had offered me early acceptance beginning January of that year, but I turned it down, wanting to finish high school with my friends and also wanting to have that time with Matt. In addition, because of my limited interactions with deaf people and my misconception that deaf people who don't speak are not as smart as deaf people who do, I felt that Gallaudet, which tended to attract deaf people who signed and didn't speak, would not be academically challenging. No one had ever explained to me that the deaf kids who don't speak, don't do so *because they weren't exposed to any language whatsoever* until they were toddlers—neither sign language nor a spoken language—and *that* affects their ability to learn. I didn't know that they were no less smart than the deaf kids who spoke, like me.

This was often the case with deaf children who had hearing parents (which is 90% of all deaf children). Things today are different, but in the past, a child's deafness often wasn't discovered until the child was diagnosed with a language delay at two or three years old. By that time, the child has gone years without any language whatsoever, which can be detrimental to the child's ability to learn.

In contrast, deaf kids born to deaf parents are usually exposed to ASL from birth, just like hearing kids are exposed to a spoken language, and they are academically on par with hearing kids or deaf kids like me who were exposed to language early on.

At the time, I didn't even realize that Gallaudet was known as the Harvard of deaf universities! At that time, Gallaudet primarily attracted deaf students who had been exposed to sign language from birth, who, unlike me, came from deaf families, and who were part of the Deaf community and Deaf Culture. Instead of going to public school, these students were often sent by their parents to residential schools for the deaf, or stay-away schools. Living in the dorms with the other deaf students and being with deaf teachers and other deaf adults, they grew up immersed in Deaf Culture and ASL.

When I arrived at NTID, it felt like Camp Mark Seven to the nth degree. I was in heaven—an entire university filled with deaf students for me to meet, hang out with, and learn from. I was back in a communication-accessible environment twenty-four hours a day; I had arrived. There were deaf dorms, professors, staff, counselors, RAs, organizations, parties, sororities, fraternities—2,000 deaf people, just like me, who brought their "being deaf" with them to explore and cultivate. I had found my niche: people to whom I could relate on all levels, people who had pride in themselves and their culture, and people whose culture was so important to them that they were full-force with it, wanting to support others on their journeys as well.

Even though most of us at NTID hadn't grown up in the Deaf community, the bond and the understanding that we all shared allowed the Deaf Culture, which we had longed for, to be easily cultivated and expressed. We inhaled it. Discovering that deafness wasn't our enemy nurtured our sense of self-acceptance and belonging. Classes and workshops on deaf-related issues and support from deaf professors helped us find our place within the Deaf community. In that milieu, I continued to evaluate myself.

My struggles with trying to fit in but feeling different in the hearing community had fueled my lifelong desire to be the best—not the best in relation to others, but the best that I could be. Now I believed that I had the *best*—the best communication, friends, teachers—everything. I was driven, aware that I was changing, but I knew that the change wasn't complete yet. I quickly became a member of the NTID Student Council. I was being propelled onward—the pull toward accepting being deaf was increasing by multitudes.

Yet, I was also in a major identity crisis, feeling angry and rebellious at my family and Matt, whom I felt didn't understand what it was like to be deaf or how important being deaf *was* to me. To be fair, even back in high school, I never *let* Matt understand, believing that if I really let go and fully embraced that I was deaf—if I went all the way and had more deaf friends and signed rather than spoke—he wouldn't be comfortable with that part of me and wouldn't want to spend his life dealing with my issues, my causes, and my world. I just focused on the present.

I was on the crest of a wave, feeling stronger than ever before, yet still not accepting of those whom I felt didn't understand me and had let me down.

When I first arrived at NTID, I was carried away with being away from home. Immersed in this newfound world, it was easy to let Matt slip from my mind. I didn't write him a single letter, and on Labor Day weekend, after having to practically force myself to go home, I saw him even though I didn't want to, and he felt my distance. Then, I played hard back at school until Thanksgiving break, when I came home and wanted to patch things up between us. But when he picked me up and we got into his car, I could tell that he wasn't himself. He was angry at me for "disappearing for months," and told me he had started dating another girl.

"It's different. We have *our song*," he said. "I really enjoy listening to the radio with her, listening to music . . ."

His words made me sick to my stomach, but I didn't say a word.

Looking back, I know that Matt didn't mean to hurt me with his comments, yet it shook me to the core because it was a sobering reminder to me that we *were* different. He was hearing and had the *right* to be hearing and enjoy those things—he *deserved* that. He didn't have to be dragged into my Deaf World and my deaf issues. He had a right to his life, as much as I had the right to mine. Even though his words felt like a slick kick in the face, they helped me to face my own truth. Never had I felt such power, yet such pain; in order to love myself, I had to lose the one I loved.

When summer came, I wrote Matt a letter; here's the gist of it:

Matt, I will always love you. But as I've grown up and entered the world, on my own, my choices for myself have changed. I am now part of the Deaf community and need a partner to share it all with me. I no longer want to stare at conversations I don't understand because people don't sign. I don't want to spend holidays at a dinner table all alone in my own world because I am not following the conversations. I no longer want to feel this terrible pull between my love for you and a world that you are not part of. Nor do I want to force you to accept a world that is not yours.

I hope that my community makes its own headlines someday, and that Deaf rights are pushed to the forefront, as we demand more awareness. Perhaps you'll read about us in the newspaper or a magazine—and even meet another deaf person. Then you might understand why it was all so important to me, and even be glad that you were not there. Brandi

Chapter Three

DEAF PRESIDENT NOW

HAVING A DEAF boyfriend helped me to adjust to NTID. To have a deaf man to walk with hand-in-hand, share meals, and have fun allowed me to begin accepting myself not only as a deaf person but also as a deaf woman in this new environment. Eric and I started dating in the midst of my self-awareness crescendo. He was 5'11", with a large build, had blonde hair and cute dimples, and was sharp as a tack. He was very involved in his fraternity, Delta Sigma Phi, so we went to frat parties all the time and hung out at the fraternity house. Although born deaf, he grew up orally, going to the Central Institute for the Deaf in St. Louis, one of the most prominent oral programs in the country. He first learned how to sign at NTID; until then, he used his voice and lip-read. His father was the president of the Clarke School for the Deaf (now, Clarke Schools for

Hearing and Speech) in Northampton, Massachusetts—the famous "oral" school that adhered to the philosophy that deaf students learn best when they can speak; they don't use sign language there at all. We were two sponges soaking up our newfound environment and embracing our newly discovered culture and identities in unison (along with everyone around us).

It was during that time that I entered and won the Miss NTID Pageant, which took place every year at the school. At the time it was a very popular event and sounded fun. What better way to explore being a deaf woman, I figured, and also have a blast. When I first arrived at NTID, I became friendly with the reigning queen, a woman named Angie, and she encouraged me to enter the pageant. I remember being so surprised that someone three years my senior would be so friendly and kind to me. She was absolutely beautiful and had the greatest smile. Angie's background was similar to mine—hearing family, oral, mainstreamed; she even grew up in the town right next to mine in the suburbs of Chicago. I felt that she had accomplished so much with her life, and she became my role model. The following spring when I became Miss NTID, she crowned me.

Pressing on with things Deaf, I signed up for the Miss Deaf Illinois state pageant that summer, the next step in the pageant circuit, which just happened to take place in my hometown of Naperville. I won that as well, and the following summer, in 1987, I became Miss Deaf Illinois. Honestly, it was great fun winning both pageants, but it was exploring myself as a deaf woman and person that was fueling me. I also have to admit that part of me still wanted to prove to my family and friends that I was capable and successful as a deaf person.

Enveloped in my new and fabulous life, I took courses on Deaf History and Culture. Somewhere along the way, I made a profound revelation: my own personal struggles over the years reflected the struggles of all deaf people— the same struggles that they had been dealing with for centuries. The world truly was contained in a single grain of sand. I could not get over what I had learned. Like most minorities, deaf people have suffered due to the ignorance, intolerance, and prejudice of others, yet there was a sad, sick, twist to our story.

Prior to 1750, the lives of people who were born deaf or became deaf prelingually were unthinkable. For thousands of years, given no exposure to any language, and therefore unable to learn, the congenitally deaf had been considered dumb or stupid. Regarded by primitive law as "incompetent," they were barred from inheriting property, marrying, receiving an education, and engaging in challenging work—all things we consider basic human rights today. The law and society treated them as idiots. They often lived alone and penniless, and were forced to do menial jobs. (I understood even more deeply why, as an oral deaf person, I thought I was too smart for the deaf program; although deaf myself, I, too, had been influenced by this horrific fallacy.)

Unable to speak and called "dumb" or "mute," deaf people couldn't communicate with their families, and except in large cities, they were cut off even from other deaf people. Having just a few simple signs and gestures, they were illiterate, considered uneducable, and lacked knowledge of the world.

Without *symbols* to represent and combine ideas, they couldn't acquire language. But the horrendous mistake—perpetuated since 355 BC when Aristotle proclaimed the deaf incapable of reason—was the idea that the symbols *had to represent speech.* The misperceptions about deaf people are ancient; the belittlement of mutes was part of the Mosaic Code, and St. Paul's pronouncement in his letter to the Romans that "faith comes by hearing," was misinterpreted for centuries to mean that the deaf were incapable of faith—and Rome wouldn't condone anyone inheriting property, if he could not give confession.

The seeds of change can be seen in the writings of Plato and in the sixteenth century when philosophers such as Jerome Cardan began questioning whether another form of language—one that involved the body—might be used to teach the deaf to communicate. Yet it wasn't until the middle of the eighteenth century, a more enlightened time generally speaking, that the future for deaf people finally became brighter. It all began when a benevolent man, the Abbé de l'Épée, became involved with the poor deaf who roamed the streets of Paris and their native sign language. Not wanting their souls to be robbed of the Catechism, de l'Épée actually *heard and then taught* them.

To everyone's surprise, by associating signs with pictures and words and using an interpreter, de l'Épée taught the deaf to read and write, and they were able to acquire an education. His school, founded in 1755, was the first school for the deaf to achieve public support. In 1791, the school became known as the National Institution for Deaf-Mutes in Paris, headed by a brilliant grammarian, the Abbé Sicard. By the time of de l'Épée's death, Sicard had established twenty-one schools for the deaf in France and Europe. Deaf schools with deaf teachers blossomed, allowing the deaf to rise from darkness and disdain to positions of eminence and responsibility—deaf philosophers, deaf writers, deaf intellectuals, deaf engineers.

This amazing change reached the United States in 1816 when Laurent Clerc (a student of one of Sicard's students), a brilliant and educated deaf man, showed American teachers the capacity for deaf people to learn when given the opportunity. With Thomas Gallaudet, Clerc set up the American Asylum for the Deaf and Dumb in Hartford, Connecticut, in 1817, and its spectacular success led to the opening of even more schools. All of the teachers of the deaf in the United States (nearly all of whom were fluent signers and many of whom were deaf) went to Hartford. Eventually, the French sign system brought over by Clerc morphed with the natal sign languages here—the deaf generate sign language wherever there are communities of deaf people—and American Sign Language (ASL) was born.

In 1864, Congress passed a law authorizing the Columbia Institution for the Deaf and Dumb in Washington, DC—now Gallaudet University—to become the first institution of higher learning specifically for the deaf. Its first principal was Edward Gallaudet, the son of

Thomas Gallaudet, who had come to the United States with Clerc. The thrust of deaf advancements continued worldwide, and the deaf were flourishing. By 1869, there were 550 teachers of the deaf around the globe and 41 percent of them were themselves deaf.

But then tragedy struck. One hundred years of advancements shriveled into nothing.

A trend toward Victorian oppressiveness and intolerances of all minorities took its toll on us, focusing particularly on our sign language. For two centuries, there had been a counteraction from teachers and parents of deaf children that the goal of education should be teaching the deaf how to speak. Questions continued being asked well into the late twentieth century as to what good the use of sign is without speech. Wouldn't it restrict deaf people to communicating only with other deaf people? Shouldn't speech and lipreading be taught, so that the deaf can integrate with the general population? Shouldn't signing be banned so that it doesn't interfere with speech?

From his travels to other deaf schools, Edward Gallaudet found (as did other experts on the deaf) that articulation skills, although very desirable, could *not* be the basis of primary teaching; this had to be achieved, and achieved early, by sign. Yet, the "oralists" worked hard to overthrow the old-fashioned sign language schools for the new progressive oralist schools, leading to the opening of the Clark School for the Deaf in Northampton, Massachusetts in 1867 (a hundred years later, Eric's father would be its president).

The most prominent oralist figure was Alexander Graham Bell, a genius whose weird family dynamics included teaching diction and correcting speech impediments (as did his father and grandfather), while at the same time denying deafness (both his mother and wife were deaf but never acknowledged this). Sickened by the idea of "a Deaf variety of the human race," he created the American Association to Promote the Teaching of Speech to the Deaf, which aimed at preventing deaf people from marrying one another, and to keep deaf students from mingling with each other. He advocated that deaf adults endure sterilization and even convinced some hearing parents to sterilize their own deaf children. Thomas Edison soon joined the cause. With Bell's power and influence behind the advocacy of oralism, the tipping point was finally reached.

In 1880, at the infamous International Congress of Education of the Deaf held in Milan, where deaf teachers were themselves excluded from the vote, the use of signing in schools was officially prohibited. To the deaf, the Milan conference's edict was like the "Jim Crow" laws to African Americans and like the ghettos to Eastern European Jews. It was a sad, sad time in Deaf History, and the anger and resentment smoldered beneath the surface until it erupted a hundred years later. Even though I had no idea at the time of my learning about it, I would soon be riding the wave of that emancipation.

The truth is that deaf people show no disposition to speak at all (except those like me who have acquired speech before becoming deaf), but they show an immediate and powerful disposition to sign—a visual language that is completely accessible to them. However, after the Milan Conference, deaf pupils could no longer use their own natural language and were forced to learn the unnatural (for them) language of speech. The proportion of deaf teachers for the deaf, which was 50 percent in 1850, fell to 25 percent by 1900 and to 12 percent by 1960. In the United States, English became the language taught to deaf students by hearing teachers, and fewer and fewer of those teachers knew sign language.

It wasn't until seventy-five years after the International Congress that things began to reverse themselves. The change was catapulted in 1955 when a linguist named William Stokoe came to Gallaudet University. He came to teach but soon realized he had so much more to accomplish. Four years later, he wrote an earth-shattering paper on sign language structure, which was the first-ever serious and scientific look at the visual language of ASL. He asserted what had always been denied: that linguistically ASL is a complete language; its syntax, grammar, and semantics are complete, although it is very different from any spoken or written language. His conclusions butted up against the long- and hard-held belief that sign language was just pantomime, namby-pamby—a pictorial language. Even *Britannica* had defined sign as "a species of picture writing in the air, more pictorial and less symbolic."

Stokoe's work was also the first to recognize the fact that deaf people had their own community, including their own language (ASL), and a history and culture that bound them together, making them different from other people (something I inherently knew but couldn't express to my family and friends). However, in its distrust of hearing people, who in the past had dictated its fate, the Deaf community took years to embrace Stokoe's work. It wasn't until the 1970s (when I became deaf) that oralism was finally being reversed, and "total communication" became accepted. Total communication is the use of both signed and spoken language, which is used at most schools today.

Still, the official sign language at that time—even at Gallaudet—was Signed Exact English (SEE) and not ASL, so deaf students were forced to learn signs for phonetic English sounds they couldn't hear. (Again this was different for me, having already learned how to speak before becoming deaf.) SEE is an exact replication of spoken English in signs and uses an English sentence structure. Actually, SEE is not considered a language in itself but rather an encoding for the English language, and it was designed with little to no input from the Deaf community. Linguists, however, consider ASL a complete language, and it is a much more intuitive way of communicating for deaf people.

Given these decades of the hearing world's deafness to the needs of the Deaf community, it isn't surprising that Gallaudet University had never had a deaf president. The only university specifically for deaf students and chartered by Congress hadn't had a deaf president since its inception 125 years earlier. In late 1987, when the university's sixth president, Jerry Lee, announced his resignation, the setting was ripe for the perfect storm.

Many factors were in play, including Stokoe's work, the formation of the National Association of the Deaf (NAD) in 1880 and other deaf advocacy organizations, and the fact that deaf people had already been running schools and had lobbying, fund-raising, and legislative experience. These factors, along with it being another progressive time in history, had the inner circles of the Deaf community thinking that the timing was right for Gallaudet University to have a deaf president. The past reticence of deaf people to advocate for themselves (tied to years of being cast aside by the hearing world) was the impetus for us to seize the moment. It was time. The university's board of directors would be making their selection in March of 1988. At the time, I was doing my stint as Miss Deaf Illinois, studying and playing hard, and I had decided to enter the Miss Deaf America Pageant.

The Deaf community as a whole wasn't quite aware of what was happening but soon would be. Behind the scenes, a few members of the Gallaudet University Alumni Association (GUAA), known as the "ducks" because they had met for the first time in a duckpin bowling alley, got to work planning a big student rally to take place a week before the election. They sent telegrams to the board of directors letting them know their position, and they joined forces with the NAD and other deaf advocacy organizations and community leaders to work together to identify, endorse, and support a deaf president. The NAD sent letters to Congress for support.

In mid-February, the presidential search committee had narrowed the candidates down to three, one hearing and two deaf, which was a victory in itself. On March 1, the student rally made it clear to the board that the Gallaudet community was insisting on the selection of a deaf president and kicked off the student's involvement. On March 5, the night before the election, the students held a candlelight vigil outside the board of director's sleeping quarters. Excitement was in the air. The students felt that a victory was at hand.

However, on Sunday, March 6, the board chose the hearing candidate, Elisabeth Ann Zinser, the vice chancellor for academic affairs at the University of North Carolina. The students closed down the school in protest. "How could this be?" the Gallaudet community exclaimed. Yeshiva University has a Jewish president; Howard University has an African American president. What's wrong with this picture? At this point, all over the country, the Deaf community was in an outrage. News of the protest was reported all week long on the six o'clock news and was on the front page of the *New York Times*.

I remember being in my dorm and reading an article in the Rochester newspaper about it on Monday, March 7, and seeing the reports on the nightly news. Because NTID was located in Rochester, the media there was always extra sensitive to deaf-related issues, so the papers covered the story very carefully. (It's hard to imagine now how we kept up with what was happening without email or smartphones.) I remember reading about the four deaf student leaders. One of them was Tim Rarus.

On the Sunday evening the board had elected Elisabeth Zinser, Tim had been doing his homework in his dorm and through his window spotted people milling about outside the university's main entrance. He went outside and saw yellow and green flyers being passed around. Everyone seemed angry and upset, and their hands were flailing a mile a minute. It was quiet pandemonium. Soon someone came over to Tim and signed, "Holy fuck," then shoved a flyer in his hand. Tim read it and then tore it into shreds. The flyer read, "The Gallaudet Board of Directors announces the election of Gallaudet University's *first woman president*"—as if putting such a positive spin on the news would somehow hide the abomination. The students had been expecting the board to formally announce their decision in person a few hours later on campus, but instead the board had issued the flyer at the last minute, only adding insult to injury.

To Tim, the announcement was like a slap in the face; it was like going back to 355 BC, when Aristotle said that deaf people were incapable of reason. Along with the rest of the students, he had been so optimistic at first because two out of the three finalists were deaf. He stood there thinking, *After all this time, nothing has changed. The board doesn't have confidence in us. They're missing the entire point. Out of three candidates—two were deaf. It was too good to be true. But they chose the hearing candidate.*

By now, faculty, staff members, and other concerned people had joined the crowd, but no one was in charge, and no one knew what to do. Gary Olsen, president of the NAD, took charge at that moment, saying that it was the *board* that was deaf because *they* hadn't listened. He told everyone to march to the Mayflower Hotel in downtown Washington, DC, where the board had been meeting, to demand an explanation. When they reached the Mayflower Hotel, word had trickled down that Jane Bassett Spilman, the chairwoman of the Gallaudet Board, had agreed to speak with three representatives inside the hotel. Someone said that the board had heard that the students were starting an uprising, and they wanted to stop it.

Tim wasn't looking to be one of the representatives— he wasn't looking for anything. However, because he was the outgoing student body government president (by one week), he was chosen, along with the new student body government president, Greg Hlibok, and a civil rights attorney (and alumnus) Jeff Rosen. The three of them went into the hotel and into one of the upstairs rooms, where Chairwoman Spilman and several other members of the Gallaudet Board—all well-respected judges, attorneys, and other professionals—along with a sign-language interpreter, were seated at a table. The three of them just stood there looking at the board members. Then Jeff Rosen blurted out, "It's bullshit," while Tim did all he could to restrain himself, and Greg Hlibok just signed, "Why?"

"The board has made their decision," the interpreter signed for the board member speaking. "Elisabeth Zinser is wonderful. She has lots of connections for fund-raising."

Although the press later reported the scandal as a possible misinterpretation, it was at that moment that Jane Spilman said: "The timing is not right for deaf people to be functioning in the hearing world," looking at no one in particular.

Their jaws dropping, Tim and his cohorts looked at each other in utter disbelief. His insides felt like they had been flipped upside down. *What have we been doing all these years, then?* he was thinking. *What has* she *been doing as our chairwoman if she doesn't think that deaf people are capable of functioning in the hearing world? The fact that* she *would even say that—isn't it her job to see that we are capable—and at Gallaudet!'* His mind was churning. *Congress has invested hundreds of millions of dollars in Gallaudet to prepare us to function in the hearing world. Obviously, the board is failing if they still have an attitude like that.*

Tim believed himself to be a reasonable guy, but *God knows, something is just wrong,* he thought. *Perhaps God also believes that it's wrong and is depending on us to make it right. Perhaps the reason the board has chosen the hearing candidate is so that deaf people finally can take their destiny into their own hands,* he pondered.

At that point, the three of them had seen just about enough; they were done. Without issuing another word, they just turned around and left, going back outside the hotel where the crowd by that point had practically doubled. Everyone was hoping that they'd talked some sense into the board. However, after hearing what had happened, the students knew that they had to just take over the situation. Their response, which in the end changed history, was a beautiful coming together process that began with the crowd leaving the Mayflower Hotel and marching to the Capitol.

The next day Tim called his grandfather—via TTY (the old teletype machines allowing deaf people to communicate from a distance)—with whom he was very close, to tell him what had happened. His grandfather didn't want him to march. *Come on! You're deaf, too,* Tim thought. *When are you going to get it?* His grandfather, like most of the elder people at the time, was afraid that Tim would be arrested and that they would lose everything they'd gained. The older people of our community were thrilled just to have jobs, TTYs, interpreting services, and captioning. They were overjoyed just to be able to drive. These things weren't possible when they were Tim's age. They treasured that there was a Gallaudet University for the deaf and that there were deaf students; they didn't want to rock the boat.

However, while Tim's generation *had* access to information, attended deaf schools, and drove cars, they also asked, "Why can't we have it all—equal access for everybody. Yes, we have a deaf university, and we need a Deaf President *Now.*" It was time to move onward. They believed that education has its place, but sometimes it just doesn't get through to people, and sometimes you have to take action. Equality for deaf people had been so long in coming that the younger generation wasn't holding back any longer.

Until Elisabeth Zinser was elected, Tim had been walking a fine line between remaining neutral (as a member of the presidential search committee—part of his job as the student body government president) and taking a stand for a deaf president. He'd been aware of all the behind-the-scenes activities and the demands that had been made on the board. Although he couldn't attend the student rally, he'd heard the buzz around campus.

"You kidding me?" people were saying. Two deaf candidates had made it to the final round. *That* was the big deal.

At the presidential search committee meetings, Tim had felt that some of the hearing committee members just weren't in tune with all of the efforts put forth by the students and alumni, such as the student rally, all the letters of support that were garnered, and their appeals to Congress. He believed that they just didn't understand the depths of what was at stake—that deaf people everywhere were insisting that Gallaudet University have a deaf president. He'd seen how awkward the dynamics in the room had been during the deaf candidate's interviews. He'd felt it. Even the few hearing members who were good signers seemed uncomfortable, standoffish, and even cold.

The truth is that the deaf candidates came in with a huge disadvantage, facing a board with seventeen hearing members and only four deaf members. Tim understood that. He understood that after centuries of misunderstandings, deaf people felt that they had to use extreme caution when talking with hearing people, especially in a situation like this. The two deaf candidates had been given the career opportunity of a lifetime—to lead Gallaudet University, with students who were deaf like them. Yet not everyone on the interview panel used ASL, so the candidates had to use a sign language interpreter instead of communicating directly in their own native language. During their interviews, not only did they have to focus on answering the questions to the best of their ability, but they also had to make sure that the interpreter both understood and then interpreted for them correctly.

Tim felt that the interpreters at the interviews did a fine job, but that the search committee members should have been sensitive to these issues, to say the very least. (This insensitivity was reflected in the final vote. Of the eighteen hearing board members only one voted for a deaf candidate, while all three deaf board members voted for a deaf candidate.) After seeing all this and then hearing Spilman's comment, Tim knew that he had to stand up and fight.

Chairman Spilman's justification for selecting Elisabeth Zinser was that she would be successful at financial networking at all levels. Tim knew that although the backbone of any successful university is the ability to acquire funds through fund-raising and Congress, the education of its students is its heart. Only a deaf president could truly understand Gallaudet's students and their needs. Tim knew with utmost certainty that it was time for Gallaudet to make its students its top priority. He was also certain that a deaf president would be just as effective in financial networking as a hearing president.

When the students returned from the Capitol, Tim and about thirty other students and supporters, including Gary Olsen, the NAD executive director, and the "ducks" came together informally and started strategizing, quickly deciding to stage a protest and determining how they would structure and represent themselves. The group later became known as the Deaf President Now (DPN) Council.

Their first task was to barricade the campus entrances (at first, they used warm bodies), so that on Monday morning, people couldn't get onto the campus. They zeroed in on their predominate message—"no deaf president, no school"—and made plans on how they'd get it across to the board, the media, and everyone else.

The DPN Council tossed ideas around and came up with four demands that the board would have to meet in order for the students to reopen the campus: the election of a Deaf President Now; the firing of Jane Spilman; the requirement that 51 percent of the Gallaudet Board be deaf, moving forward; and that there be no reprisals against the students, faculty, and staff involved.

Tuesday evening, in front of a packed gym, Tim signed passionately about the power behind what they were doing, sharing how much it personally meant to him to fight for what he deeply believed in. He cheered the students on for finally standing up for themselves and demanding a *Deaf President Now*, the student's motto during the protest and their cry for freedom. He reinforced the mandate that the students keep the school closed until the board agreed to all four of their demands, and he asked them where else, other than at Gallaudet, the heart of the Deaf community, would change of this magnitude be initiated. The other three leaders, Greg Hlibok, Bridgetta Bourne, and Jerry Covell, also spoke about the Gallaudet community's commitment to do or die on this issue.

The press was everywhere, as were the interpreters for them, wearing armbands made of masking tape so that they could be easily recognized. (The media's inexperience in dealing with the deaf showed, as they had to be directed not to give the microphone to the deaf speaker but to his or her interpreter.) It was a tremendous time for Tim but also incredibly stressful with people needing things from him left and right. Like many others, Tim only slept a few hours that week and stole naps whenever he could. Although stressed and tired, a force much greater than he realized was moving Tim and this movement forward.

By Wednesday, things began falling into place; Congress threatened to cut off the funding to Gallaudet if there wasn't a resolution. The issue was no longer gray, but black and white—the election of the hearing candidate was an act of discrimination! People all over the nation—deaf, hearing, black, white, disabled, fully functioning, young, and old—began seeing the situation in commonsense terms. Tim clarified it for all that evening in an interview by Tom Brokaw on the national news (Brokaw was in New York City while Tim was in Georgetown in the District of Columbia). Although he was extremely nervous—after all, he'd be live on television where there was no room for screwups—Tim spoke about the discrimination of the deaf to the entire country.

To the millions of people watching, he said that the uprising at Gallaudet was like a deaf Selma, Alabama, and he compared Jane Spilman's horrendous comment to when Rosa Parks in 1955 was asked to go to the back of the bus because she was African American. "Rosa Parks refused to be discriminated against," he said looking straight into the camera, ". . . and deaf people refuse, too." During another television interview, he simply turned to the cameras and said, "No deaf president, no university." He was insisting on an end to this "client mentality," where deaf people are willing to be clients of their hearing masters when they should be controlling their own destiny, and that deaf people will no longer be passive and accept this kind of treatment from the hearing culture. That week, Tim was interviewed several times by local television stations and newspapers, as were many others.

Later that same evening, Greg Hlibok was interviewed by Ted Koppel on *Nightline*, along with Elisabeth Zinser and Marlee Matlin, who said Zinser should resign. At that point, Zinser was still holding a hard line (the board's original strategy) that the board had chosen her to be the university's leader and had confidence in her ability. I remember Ted Koppel asking her point blank if she were a puppet of the board.

But too much momentum had already built up against Zinser for her to remain strong. I. King Jordan, the remaining deaf candidate (the other had withdrawn from the race) who had also originally supported the board's selection of a hearing president, retracted his support, saying that he stood with the students and with the Deaf community. His retraction reenergized the students, as well as the Deaf community at large. With all the media attention the students' cause was getting and the outpouring of support for them from every direction, Thursday evening while at a meeting together, Elisabeth Zinser looked at

Jane Spilman and simply said, "I resign." She did this with amazing grace, saying that she couldn't run the university without support from the faculty and that she didn't want to stand in the way of "such a monumental event in Deaf Culture."

At DPN headquarters that evening, at 11:00, Tim and a few others read the press release announcing Zinser's resignation. They went wild, hugging, lifting each other up, and giving double high-fives. It was surely a victory; however, much more still needed to be accomplished.

The following morning, our two NTID buses rolled into Washington, DC. The NTID Student Congress (of which I was a representative at large) had used money from their budget to take students to Gallaudet so that they could join the march to the Capitol. Way before Zinser had resigned, the Gallaudet students had planned Friday's march to be the big finale; politicians, community leaders, and students were all scheduled to speak out in unison. Eric and I had boarded the bus at midnight the night before, which drove through the night and arrived at Gallaudet that morning around 8:00 AM. Our bus had signs on the windows that read, *Honk for a Deaf President*, as did the signs on cars and that people were carrying everywhere. Of course, we didn't hear the honking, but we felt it. It was then that we learned of Zinser's resignation. The motto that spread through the campus in the aftermath was, "Three and a half more demands to go."

It was the perfect day for a march to the Capitol; we could not have been blessed with better weather.

The beautiful day matched the energy on the Gallaudet Campus, which I felt the minute I walked through the main entrance gates. People were cooking and selling "Spilmandogs" and "Boardburgers." At one point, I watched the members of the American Postal Workers Union give a check to the Gallaudet students in support. We hung around, meeting and talking with people, until it was time for the march. Despite being up all night, I was feeling more alive than I can say.

At the helm, the four student leaders carried a sign that said, "We Still Have A Dream," the same banner carried by civil rights leaders in their efforts to have Martin Luther King's birthday declared a national holiday, borrowed from

ERIC AND ME MARCHING TO THE CAPITOL

the Crispus Attucks Museum of Washington, DC. As Tim and his cohorts led the way, he started tasting victory. He felt as if he'd been in the middle of the jungle for years, pushing, pushing, pushing back the brush until finally he pushed back that last bit and saw what he had been missing all along. His dream of freedom for deaf people, he believed, might finally be coming true.

The march was the DPN's grand opus, which culminated at the Capitol, as Tim and the other three leaders led three thousand of us through neighborhood upon neighborhood, many of which were African American. People were outside their homes just cheering us on. The press was there in droves. Signs were being waved everywhere saying just about anything you can imagine: "Zinserbusters," "Deaf Prez Now," "Spilman is not ready for the Deaf World," to name just a few.

Finally, we turned down Pennsylvania Avenue, walking together as one. Eric and I could just feel the power. Actually, the energy among us was very exciting yet peaceful, sort of how I'd imagined Woodstock might have been. I felt like the whole country was there. A young woman and her grandmother were walking next to us—they were hearing. An older deaf couple was walking right behind us. There were Caucasians, African Americans, women wheeling their babies in strollers, people in wheelchairs, Asians, Hispanics, and even dog owners and their dogs. People of every possible race, nationality, and lifestyle were there—all marching for us and marching for freedom.

Finally, we arrived at the Capitol. I was most inspired by seeing so many eloquent, passionate speeches coming from people my own age. We had come so far in such a short amount of time. However, at day's end, the board still hadn't met three of the four student demands, and no one knew what the board would decide.

For Tim, this really was the day when deaf people were finally liberated from the chains placed on them by the hearing world. Standing in front of the Capitol, he looked out on our sea of diversity—three thousand of us there solely to support him and the other leaders in whatever they would say. In the past, whenever Tim had spoken to large groups, he was afraid that he'd feel awkward, but that day he knew that whatever he said, people would hoot and holler in support. As everyone waved their hands wildly as he signed to them, he thought, *Is this really happening? Am I dreaming? Have we finally seen the light?*

I had my own epiphany.

What we had accomplished was a triumph for the Deaf community; walking hand-in-hand, we showed the entire world that deaf people would no longer allow others to set limits on what we can achieve. We were an impressive group, indeed. Many African Americans living in Washington, DC, who had seen the Deaf community as "white" and not as a group that, like them, had been discriminated against, began seeing us in a new light. Equality was in the air. Standing before the Capitol, I knew that no matter how different we were from one another, we were also the same, sharing the same basic human needs and deserving of the same basic human rights. It was an experience beyond my wildest dreams and the pinnacle of my life.

That afternoon, all of the things that I'd been saying all those years to my family, friends, and to Matt, specifically, were finally validated. Any resentment I'd felt toward them for pushing aside and not comprehending my feelings or for invalidating me by saying, "Oh, Brandi, you're just like us"—for trying to put a positive spin on an attitude that was incredibly oppressive—was validated. I knew that they loved and cared about me, but their "support" had made me feel like I was somebody I wasn't.

I finally had a voice and realized deeper still that I hadn't been crazy—being deaf *was* different and had been isolating. All of my trials had been worth it. Father Tom's wise words had started my journey to Washington, DC, and had led me to that very moment when I finally knew that I hadn't been wrong all along. When the board announced on Sunday evening the election of I. King Jordan as Gallaudet University's first deaf president, I was ecstatic and at peace with myself and the world.

My experiences had changed me, opened me to a new world and culture, and even though I didn't want being deaf to limit or define me (like my camp counselor Carla had said), it was steadily becoming an integral part of who I was. The Deaf community had become an extension of my own family, giving me a great sense of connected-ness and belonging. Even back then, before smartphones, BlackBerrys, and videophones had leveled the playing field—enabling us to communicate with each other and with the rest of the world as easily as hearing people—our networking was unbelievable. All the deaf in America were now in one gated community, founded on a deep need and desire for connection with one another. I saw myself as a unique person within the community and part of a culture that I thought was so unbelievably beautiful.

TIM AND THE OTHER THREE DPN STUDENT LEADERS—BRIDGETTA BOURNE, (TO TIM'S RIGHT) GREG HLIBOK, AND JERRY COVELL—SPEAKING TO THE CROWD AT THE CAPITOL AFTER THE MARCH

Chapter Four

FULL CIRCLE

I N THE SPRING of 1988, after becoming Miss Deaf Illinois, I went for broke and entered the Miss Deaf America Pageant—again, mostly for the fun of it. However, after the protest happened, it quickly began to dawn on me that the Miss Deaf America Pageant was about a lot more than fun and games. Deaf people had just moved mountains. Although a long time coming, our new world seemed to be created in seven days, or at least its beginnings. Our spirits were high, and we felt super great about ourselves. The coverage of the protest had struck a chord with hearing people, pointing out our discrimination and grabbing their attention. For the first time ever, they were interested in us and our cause. I figured it would be a very good time to represent deaf Americans. Whoever became Miss Deaf America would be representing deaf people to the country and to the world.

Back then, the pageant was always a highly visible event in the Deaf community and would be even more so with all that had recently happened. The pageant was an expression of our culture and community and, now, our newfound liberation. The winner would tour the country as an ambassador for the NAD, the pageant's sponsor. I have to say that, as an adult, I've always been extremely uncomfortable talking about that part of my life, let alone writing about it in a book. I think it's partly because pageants today are not what they were two decades ago. Back then, there were very few female role models, so young girls would look to the Miss America Pageant as something they could become. That no longer rings true because now we have women in top positions everywhere—from CEOs to politicians running for president of our country.

Yet truth be told, besides all the fanfare and fun, my experience thrust me into the very heart of the Deaf community and also brought me gifts beyond compare. The event was not a beauty pageant or popularity contest. There was no swimsuit competition, so it wasn't about sex appeal, and more than half our score was based on intensive interviews. My experience not only deepened my understanding of what it meant to be deaf and strengthened my Deaf Pride, but it also helped me trust in a higher power or "goodness" that set my life on fire. My experiences as Miss Deaf America led me into a wonderful career in telecommunications, meeting and marrying Tim, having three beautiful sons, and adopting Zoe, who, bless her heart, would be the real beneficiary of all that I had learned. And, it was a wonderful time in my life.

I never thought in a million years that after competing as Miss Deaf Illinois, I'd go on to become Miss Deaf America. Just being one of the finalists, to me, would have meant that I'd really accomplished something. Well, I *did* think that I could win—I had a lot of confidence in my presentation; it was just that I was so sure that Angie, who was Miss Deaf Connecticut, would win.

During the week of the pageant, my chaperone and I roomed together, as did the other contestants and their chaperones, at the Hilton Hotel in Charleston, South Carolina, where the pageant finals would take place on Friday evening. We had all arrived several days earlier to compete in the preliminary competitions. Happily, I started out with a bang by winning the preliminary talent performance, interpreting the poem, "Oh God, I Am Only Seventeen," which often appeared in the Ann Landers column in newspapers around graduation time, reminding teenagers not to drink and drive. The theater teacher at NTID had coached me all year in preparation. During the private interview, which counted for 35 percent of our score, I was asked about the Gallaudet Protest, my most positive experiences as a deaf person, and if I thought that ASL should be taught to all deaf children, to which, of course, I said yes.

It was an exciting yet incredibly stressful time. The media was creating a big buzz only months after Gallaudet. I was running on adrenaline and hardly any sleep and was so nervous that I could hardly eat. I wanted to do well more than anything and wasn't sure if I would. Meanwhile, my mother, father, brother, grandmother, aunt, uncle, and Eric would all be there Friday night rooting for me, and I didn't want to disappoint them.

Finally, Friday evening arrived. Our opening number was a dance, but because I can't keep a beat to save my life, I just winged it. I thought that I was awful, but I guess it wasn't being judged. Right after we finished, they announced the ten finalists, and, to my delight, I was one of them. At that point, our scores were wiped clean except for the private interview score from the preliminaries.

For the on-stage interview question (which was designed to show the judges how well we could think on our feet), we were asked how we might preserve our Deaf Culture. I responded by saying, "We preserve our culture by educating our Deaf children about our culture, and by celebrating who and what we are, just like we did at the Gallaudet Protest." It amazes me now just to think about how prescient my own words were for what the future had in store for me.

When the interviews were finally over, it was time to announce the winners. The ten of us stood in a line, each incredibly nervous and excited, facing an audience of about one thousand. After they announced the third, second, and the first runners-up, five of us remained, including Angie, who was next to me. The stillness in the auditorium was palpable. After a maddening pause, the emcee continued, ". . . and the new Miss Deaf America of 1988 is . . . Miss Deaf

Top ten finalists at the Miss Deaf America Pageant. My good friend, Anne Marie, Miss Deaf Minnesota and first runner up, is on my left.

Illinois." At first, I just couldn't believe it. I was stunned, but recovered quickly and then gave Angie a huge hug. Afterward, there was a beautiful reception for all of the contestants and their family members, along with representatives of the NAD and other VIPs.

And so it began. I was the keynote speaker at NAD state association banquets, conferences, and pageants. I spoke at corporations and deaf schools—both residential, stay-away schools, which deaf students from deaf families often go to, and public schools with deaf programs similar to the one I had attended. I learned about the laws relating to education and about my rights as a deaf person, such as Public Law 94-142, which is a plan that helps children with special needs participate in school. I learned about the Americans with Disabilities Act (ADA), which hadn't yet been passed but soon would be, thanks to a push from the Gallaudet Protest. I learned about our right to have interpreters and closed-captioning for TV, and a whole world opened up for me regarding the ways that technology could make deaf people's lives a lot easier and more enjoyable (and back then technology was nothing like it is today).

I signed the national anthem at a Chicago Cubs baseball game and, at the college level, for Fresno State in California, among other teams. I never liked performing those musical numbers though. I couldn't really feel the rhythm and didn't feel confident in my performance. Public speaking was more my strength, and due to the Gallaudet Protest, I had many more requests to give speeches and talks than prior Miss Deaf Americas. I went from city to city, encountering so many different people, places, and experiences. Only occasionally, I felt a little sad thinking about my friends partying back at school and the fun I was missing out on.

One of my advisors from school, Tom Holcomb, helped me with the content and ideas to use when developing my presentations and talks. In my travels, I gave workshops or speeches on "Deafness 101" and "Deaf Culture in the Workplace," where I shared how employers can create a positive environment for their deaf employees by providing interpreters, TTYs (Text Telephones), and occasionally having silent lunches where no one speaks but instead practices signing. "Disability Awareness Week" was a very busy travel time for me. I spoke at dozens of large corporations and agencies, including Bell Labs (AT&T), the Social Security Administration, and the Department of Transportation, to name just a few. Because I wanted to be sure that people understood everything I said, as a rule I used interpreters to voice for me when I gave my presentations, and used my own voice when I was talking one-on-one or with family and friends.

For me, though, the most fulfilling and humbling part of being Miss Deaf America was visiting the deaf schools or mainstreamed programs and having those sweet little kids look up to me as a role model. I remember once, when I was six months into my reign and had come home for winter break, several of the local schools had scheduled appearances for me, including one elementary school with a deaf program very similar to the one I had gone to. I spoke at their all-school assembly, which had both deaf and hearing students attending, and talked about what it was like to be deaf, the kind of technology we used to assist us, and how cool sign language was, and I answered questions from the audience.

After the assembly, I visited a third-grade deaf classroom where the kids had made me cards to thank me for coming. One adorable little boy with red hair and dimples handed me his card. On the front, he had drawn balloons next to a girl who was wearing a dress and a crown. Inside the card, he had drawn smiles next to his note. As I read it, he looked up at me with his big brown eyes. It said, "Dear Miss Deaf America, I am sorry you are deaf."

Whoa. I was right back at camp with Father Tom. My heart ached for him, for me, for every person who had ever felt unworthy. I kneeled down next to him and signed, "You are sorry that I am deaf?"

"Yes," he signed, not at all upset. It was probably an attitude picked up in the schoolyard.

"No. You must not be sorry," I responded. "I am not sorry. Look at me. I am doing well. I am in college. I am happy. I am Miss Deaf America. Being deaf is a great thing, and it's great for you, too. Do not be sorry!"

He just looked at me and nodded, then gave me a big hug. I don't know what happened to that little boy, but he represented the epitome of my two years as Miss Deaf America. I realized then how very important it was that mainstreamed deaf kids, or any deaf kids for that matter, felt proud of who they are and of our culture.

Ironically, the first big assignment during my reign, given to me about two weeks after I was crowned, was attending a conference at the AG Bell Association. The AG Bell Association is an "oralist" organization comprised of doctors, speech therapists, and audiologists—all hearing professionals, who like their founder, Alexander Graham Bell, believed in "oralism"—that teaching deaf children how to speak was the best way to raise them. Eric's father, who, in addition to being the president of the Clarke School for the Deaf, was also the president of AG Bell, invited me to attend, so Eric and I went together.

There was a political issue there. The NAD (whom I was representing) and the AG Bell Association, while politically friendly, had very different philosophies on deaf education. The NAD, founded by deaf people and representing the Deaf community, strongly advocated the use of ASL and discouraged oralism. In fact, there was a big to-do in the Deaf community that Miss Deaf America was dating the son of the president of the AG Bell. I remember being so surprised initially that the NAD had decided to send me. Perhaps, it was a gesture of goodwill.

However, no sooner had Eric and I arrived at the conference, than the buzzing began, "Look, Eric, the president's son is signing instead of speaking," people were saying.

Soon Eric's father, who performed the opening ceremony, began speaking. After a few opening remarks, he scanned the room until he found Eric sitting next to me and then locked his eyes on him and said, "Many of you know my son, Eric, who is a criminal justice major at the National Technical Institute of the Deaf. He is deaf and signs. I am not upset that Eric signs, nor am I upset that he has chosen to live in the world of the Deaf. But when he was a child, I wanted to be sure that later on he would be able to make that choice for himself. Today Eric chooses when to speak and when to sign; that is his choice to make."

His words reverberated through me as if I somehow knew that I would be making a similar decision one day, but it wasn't until many, many years later that I fully appreciated why.

My next assignment about two months after that landed me at Gallaudet University at the biggest celebration ever to take place in the school's history. It was a triple whammy: the inauguration of I. King Jordan, the school's 125th anniversary, and homecoming weekend—all rolled up into one big fête. The spirit at the school was still soaring. Gallaudet had its first deaf president—it was an immeasurable morale boost! A big parade was scheduled to kick off the festivities, and I was invited, as Miss Deaf America, to sit in a car with the student government president and the homecoming king and queen.

Tim Rarus was the homecoming king.

I remembered seeing him on television being interviewed by Tom Brokaw and how taken I had been with his passion and energy, his beautiful signing, and how inspiring he had been at the Capitol. He was easy on the eyes, too. That's why I was completely shocked when he didn't sign a single word to me the entire time we sat next to each other in the car. Not even a hello. I was invisible to him. I thought that he was cute and was attracted to his energy and air of confidence. However, I couldn't get over how a person could be so rude. I just couldn't fathom it, so I wasn't about to admit to myself that I admired him.

It wasn't until several months later that I realized that he felt that I was too "oral" for him. Tim was one of the many culturally deaf people of that era who didn't socialize with deaf people who spoke and didn't use ASL—some were pretty militant about it. Even though I signed, I used a version of SEE (Signed Exact English), which is different

ME AND TIM IN GALLAUDET PARADE CAR. TIM WAS THE HOMECOMING KING.

from ASL. We understood each other fine; we just didn't express ourselves in the same mode of sign language. Yet, to Tim, I may as well have been a foreigner with a different language, culture, customs, and way of thinking.

Back then, most oral people, like me, wanted to engage more significantly with the culturally deaf, but not all of them wanted to mingle with us. Later, when Tim and I first began dating, some of his friends had a real problem accepting me. They gave me the sign, *hearing-minded*, which means someone who is hearing, but it's all in the head—in other words, a deaf person who tries to pass off as hearing. It's not a positive comment. At first, it really bothered me, and I tried so hard to prove that I wasn't hearing-minded, but eventually I came to my senses, realized it was a xenophobic label, and chose to ignore it.

Even though Tim ignored me, I let bygones be bygones. However, the following spring, he brushed me off again at a reception on Capitol Hill that was being sponsored by Tony Coelho, a Democratic congressman from California and a primary sponsor of the ADA. The reception was in honor of me, as Miss Deaf America, and I. King Jordan, and it was sponsored by the NAD and NTID. The incident happened while Tim was on the receiving line, where people first shook hands with I. King Jordan's wife, then I. King Jordan, and then me. Tim shook their hands and then walked off. *Strike two,* I thought.

The following summer, our paths crossed yet again when I was asked to speak at the Youth Leadership Camp (YLC) located in Pengilly, Minnesota, also sponsored by the NAD. YLC attracts the brightest deaf children from all over the country and teaches them leadership skills by introducing them to leaders in the Deaf community. Tim was working there as the Dean of Boys. After arriving at camp, I went into the dining hall and saw Tim sitting at a table eating. Our eyes met, but that was the extent of our interaction.

Later that evening, after making a presentation to the campers, I joined the staff at a bar in town. There must have been twenty of us sitting around the table. Tim was sitting directly across from me, but at first we didn't speak to each other. One by one people began leaving, and when only four of us remained, he and I started talking. After about ten minutes I just looked at him and said, "I have to tell you that I really don't like you."

"Don't like me?" he said.

"No. You were very rude to me the last two times we met."

"I was?" he said, genuinely surprised. It was then that I realized that he hadn't been trying to be a smart-ass or be mean or rude to me that day in the parade car. Because of his background, it's like he didn't even see me. It's just that I was everything he wasn't. Mainstreamed. Oral. I had a hearing family and had gone to NTID instead of to Gallaudet. I didn't use ASL. He wasn't interested in people like me. I didn't fit into his world.

"Yes, you were rude," I continued. "We sat in that car for over an hour, and you didn't say a single word to me." Then I said, "I don't know what *you* call that, but I call it rude." He didn't miss a beat.

"A strong girl. I like that," he said. "Thanks for your honesty. I will try to do better next time," he promised with a huge grin on his face, as if he were totally amused by me.

For the remainder of the evening, I could feel the attraction between us and left the bar not sure of what had happened, but knowing that something had. The next morning when I saw him in the administrator's cabin, I felt butterflies in my stomach.

"Good morning," he said to me.

"Good morning, Tim."

"I just want to point out that I said, 'good morning' and am not being rude to you today," he continued, that adorable grin back on his face.

"Good for you. You just earned a brownie point," I shot back.

After that, I was keenly aware of his presence whenever he was around me during the day. When we made eye contact, it was electric. I knew he was watching me. He knew I was watching him. After seventy-two hours, we were together, just like that. Like fate, we started a conversation and never stopped. A few days later, while we were in the dining room eating lunch, he teased me, saying that he had been in the audience at the Miss Deaf America Pageant rooting for the Gallaudet contestants.

"Yeah, well, I bet you're glad that I won now."

I was scheduled to stay at camp for three days, but ended up staying for two weeks until the summer ended, as "friend of the Dean." Tim drove me home to Naperville, where I stayed with my mother for a week and then told her that I was driving back to school with friends but, instead, drove to Washington, DC, to be with Tim. He had just graduated from Gallaudet the previous May and had taken a job working for John McCain, whom he met through DPN (Deaf President Now), and who represented his home state of Arizona.

Before leaving, I met Matt at Friday's Restaurant, where we used to go. While we weren't "together" anymore, we'd left things open, never saying that we were "finished." We had stayed in touch over the years, seeing each other when we could. That night we had another conversation about our deaf and hearing issues, and, again, he tried to reason with me. But by then, I was crystal clear that I would not compromise my communication. Matt's family and friends were all hearing. I wanted my deafness to be a *part of who I was*. I didn't want to have to choose anymore. With Tim, I didn't have to.

He was everything I ever wanted. He was handsome, charming, and the *epitome* of deafness—the personification of the world and culture for which I'd been yearning. I'd never met anyone so motivated, passionate, and knowledgeable about deaf people and Deaf rights. I admired that. Tim was a fixture in the Deaf community. Almost everyone I met in my travels as Miss Deaf America knew him. Half of them had said to me, "Sure, I know Tim. I changed his diaper." I remember thinking, *What?* But that's the Deaf community. Because Tim's mother was a strong deaf advocate when he was a child, she took him with her to deaf events all the time, so he grew up as one of the community's children.

Through his actions and words, Tim validated my thinking and concerns about being deaf and about how deaf people truly were and should be treated. From the moment of his birth, he was immersed in Deaf Culture. Tim's family was in that small 10 percent of the population where both the parents *and* the child are deaf. He had come from *four generations* of deafness—his parents, grandparents, and great-grandparents on his mother's side all were deaf. His sister was deaf.

Tim's grandfather, mother, and stepfather were all strong deaf advocates and had been on the NAD Board of Directors for years, so there was always political talk going on at his house. As Miss Deaf America, I represented the NAD, so when we sat down to dinner, I could relate and felt included and accepted.

Being with Tim's family was like being in a Deaf Mecca, from the way that they signed to their involvement in deaf advocacy, from their awareness about their rights as deaf people to their unequivocal sense of belonging to and believing in the Deaf community, which was like their family. I was new to the scene, and it was all so powerful and moving to me. Awestruck as I was, I felt right at home because they were all so warm and accepting. More than that, I felt like *I* had found a new family. It was because of hanging around with them that I just naturally changed my signing style from SEE to using more ASL.

SEE is based on English grammar and is not at all like that painting-a-picture kind of signing that you see with ASL. For example, when Tim tells a story, he brings such fullness to his descriptions. They're visualized with details that are hard to capture using written English and would be rare for someone who's reciting a story. Everything is placed, the whole scene is set up, and you can see where everyone and everything is. Because Tim thinks visually, as do most deaf people, ASL is a much more intrinsic, intuitive way of communicating for him. The emotions and grammar of what he is saying are expressed not only through signs but also through his movements and facial expressions, just as they are expressed through a person's vocal intonations in spoken English. Tim brings his humor and his entire personality to whatever he is saying.

Being with Tim's family made me realize just how different his upbringing was from mine. To have actually grown up in a family that had total, unlimited communication was astounding to me. I remembered sitting in the movie theaters with my friends and in church feeling so different and isolated. Tim always had an interpreter at church and always went to the captioned movies (whatever few there were). I was amazed by how our experiences of learning about ourselves and the world were so different.

As a child, Tim didn't even realize that he was different from most people. His parents had told him about the big, wide, hearing world out there, and he knew that all of his neighbors were hearing, but it had no meaning for him; he was just busy playing and being a kid. *Yeah, they're hearing, whatever,* he thought.

As Tim grew older, his mother told him about the barriers that deaf people had faced in the past—how they couldn't drive or get jobs and had to depend on hearing people for just about everything. Prior to the 1960s, before there were TTYs, if deaf people wanted to call a doctor, for example, either they had to walk or drive to a hearing neighbor's house and have the neighbor make the call for them, or drive to the house of a deaf friend who had a hearing child. The TTY brought us independence and freedom; now, just like the rest of the hearing world, we could finally stay home and call our friends and families. Later, when the ADA was passed, it required the usage of Telecommunications Relay Services (TRS), which came before the Video Relay Services (VRS) that we use today.

TRS was a telephone system that allowed people with TTYs to connect to an operator who would then relay their communication to hearing callers who did not have a TTY. But even with the TTY, communication was limited, at best. The need for connection and communication has always been so paramount for us because we've never had enough of it.

Tim's mother kept telling him that things had become so much better for deaf people, and he was happy to be living in such good times. His mother really amazed me. She was the first deaf principal at the Arizona School for the Deaf, where Tim attended, at a time when neither deaf nor hearing women held key administrative positions. Because Tim's grandfather was a strong advocate for the deaf, she, too, would become a fervent advocate and educator in her own right. Just like Tim's grandfather, she believed that both deaf and hearing people had to be educated about one another.

In the 1980s, she spearheaded a group in Tucson, Arizona, that was raising money to build a Deaf community center. To acquire funds for the people she was representing, his mother testified before a group of hearing mayors and commissioners, saying that there needed to be a place where deaf people could assemble and that if they didn't support their project, it would be like going back to Greek and Roman times when deaf people were thrown into prison and forgotten about.

Yet it was Tim's grandfather who stood out as his hero in his family because of all that he had accomplished. His grandfather had put himself through graduate school, earning three degrees without any support whatsoever at a time when deaf people didn't have access to interpreters or notetakers—it was unprecedented. The man knew four different languages, including sign language, and he also lip-read. Tim's parents had divorced when he was six, so his grandfather became a surrogate father to him. Throughout his childhood, he heard stories about his grandfather's political involvements—how he had lobbied for the NAD at state associations and conferences, particularly in New Jersey where he lived, and for the National Fraternal Society of the Deaf, an organization that helped deaf people get car insurance. Back in the 1970s, although it was legal for deaf people to drive, insurance companies wouldn't sell them car insurance. His grandfather was also the founder and president of the New Jersey Association of the Deaf. Tim saw him educating people by explaining who deaf people were and how they did things. He listened to his grandfather tell stories about how deaf people had been put in jail for months for crimes they hadn't committed and didn't receive due process or have interpreters at their trials.

Despite his lack of access to information, despite having to work three times harder than his hearing counterparts while in school and at work because he didn't have an interpreter (he was the only deaf employee at AT&T), and despite being treated like a second-class citizen at restaurants, hotels, and other public places his entire life, he never complained and was grateful for what had been given him. He wanted Tim to appreciate all that he had, as well, which was why he was against him marching at Gallaudet. He told Tim that he had to try harder and had to "earn his keep" with hearing people—that to achieve his goals and make his way in the world, he had to listen better and have better relationships with the people around him. He told Tim to jump into situations and work them out—that there were no shortcuts—and that he had to respect that process. Above all, he taught Tim to respect his elders.

It took some time for Tim to see the wisdom in his grandfather's ways, and until then he idolized him and yearned for his approval, but felt like he could never be like him or live up to his standards. When we achieved our victory at Gallaudet, his grandfather said to him, "You were right, my grandson." Tim felt like he was finally becoming a man who would make his grandfather proud.

It was through pure osmosis and because of his intelligence, decency, and passionate nature that Tim's intolerance for inequity and need to stand up and fight for what he believed in became a thread in his being and a guiding principle in his life.

It started way back in preschool when he had to wear a horrid device that helped him to practice speaking—a black box that had two cords coming out in front of him. Back in the early 70s, even though students at the deaf schools signed with each other and with their teachers, the emphasis was still on speech reading. At the American School for the Deaf, which Tim attended through fourth grade, it was the same thing; they used speech very often as a means to communicate.

Oh, it made his blood boil. His teachers would smoke and drink coffee and make him say, "M" or "B" with a feather in front of his mouth. They'd tell him, "Say, 'in, in' like this. It's with your nose," then the following day tell him that it didn't sound right. He did it over and over again. He saw no value in saying letters he couldn't hear.

When he was older, he'd go out to eat with his mother, sister, and grandparents, and his grandmother always told him, "Ssshhh, keep it down. Sign small, sign small," not wanting people to notice them. Tim thought, *What's wrong with us? Why are we hiding this? If hearing people have a problem with it, it's their problem, not ours.* Then he'd sign bigger and bigger, using an eighteen-inch sign box, figuring that you couldn't get any bigger than that.

Tim's mother always told him that being deaf was a full-time job and that a lot of work still needed to be done, and it struck him deeply to keep educating and keep advocating. It became clear to him that even though deaf people needed the support of hearing people, we had to decide for ourselves what was best for us. A passion was ignited in him to embrace the challenges that would come his way.

In 1997, six years after we were married, representing the Committee for the Deaf and Hard of Hearing, he stood before one of the Senate committees, pointing out the inequity between deaf and hearing people regarding the use of the telephone. (At the time, telephone service was relatively inexpensive for hearing people but expensive for deaf people.) This inequity was partly due to the way that a particular law had been written concerning equipment used in conjunction with telephone networks (such as a telephone, TTY, or amplified phone for the hard of hearing).

But videophones, used by deaf people, required an Internet connection, so the law had to be rewritten to also make it apply to them, reducing the costs of their equipment (which was $900 then compared to $200 or even less today). To change the way the law was written, the proposed change had to go through one of the Senate committees, whose approval was needed before it was brought to the floor for both Houses to vote on. If this law was passed, deaf and hearing people would finally be on equal footing regarding telephone usage.

Tim stood before the committee, which was entirely hearing, and, via his interpreter, asked everyone in the audience to raise their hand if they used a telephone. They all thought he was crazy. He saw everyone looking around the room to see who else had raised their hand. After everyone's hands were raised, Tim explained that deaf people deserved the same access to the telephone as hearing people—that we, too, should be able to raise our hands.

However, it was about a year after we had started dating that Tim reaped the fruits of all his advocacy—in the past and in the future—this time not at the Capitol but on the South Lawn of the White House. He'd been working for John McCain for about a year and had worked his way up from the mailroom to being involved with disability rights and the ADA. It was summer, and he was the camp director at YLC, when he got a call from McCain, who then flew him from Minnesota to Washington, DC. On July 26, 1990, he and several other McCain staffers and legislators rode in a van to the White House South Lawn and watched President H. W. Bush sign the ADA into law.

The bill had been submitted twice before but hadn't passed. However, this time when it was submitted, Justin Dart, an activist for people with disabilities who worked with President Bush, mentioned the Gallaudet Protest in their appeal to Congress, helping the bill to finally be passed. The chief sponsor of the act was Senator Tom Harkin, who had a deaf brother and was very passionate about the issue. Harkin garnered support from different senators, including John McCain, to help write some of the titles in the Act: McCain worked on Title IV while Tim was working for him.

Title IV concerned traditional relay services, which laid the foundation for Video Relay Services that today allow both deaf and hearing people to have equal access to the telephone. (Deaf people use videophones that require an Internet connection.) If it hadn't been for the passing of the ADA, Tim and I probably wouldn't have careers in video communications today.

A few weeks after the bill was passed, we became engaged. It happened on the night that I crowned the new Miss Deaf America in Indianapolis. I didn't think that as Miss Deaf America it would be appropriate to be engaged, which Tim understood. However, the minute I put that crown on the girl's head, he was waiting for me outside the convention hall with a horse and carriage, little roses strewn all around inside. He proposed as we rode around the city.

Eric and I had parted ways earlier that spring, realizing that we were better off as friends. I wrote Matt, who I hadn't seen in about a year, and told him of my engagement. Since our relationship had been such an important part of both our lives, I felt it was the right thing to do. I wrote, "Someday when I have a daughter with a love of her own, our story will always be one I tell her. I hope she will know a first love as great as ours."

A year after that Tim and I were married. Father Tom performed our marriage ceremony. I flew him from New York to Naperville, and, in front of 150 people, he married us in my church. What a gift it was to be able to say my vows to Tim directly, one-on-one, in ASL, without having to say them through a third party. The interpreter was there for the hearing people.

I had come full circle from the time, seven years earlier, when I had sat by the water listening to Father Tom. Back then, I couldn't have even imagined where my life would lead me. Standing before me was the man who had helped me begin my journey to self-acceptance; he was marrying me to the man who had helped me arrive. I felt free, accepting of myself as I truly was. My identity crisis was over, replaced by a sense of power and joy.

ME, TIM, FATHER TOM (left), AND FATHER JERRY (right) AT OUR WEDDING

The following fall, Tim and I moved to Kansas City, Kansas, where I began working for Sprint Communications and Tim began working for Gallaudet University as the assistant director of the Gallaudet Regional Center there. He wanted to have children right away. While I cherished the idea of having children, especially a daughter, the timing just didn't seem right. I couldn't possibly have known the lengths to which I'd have to go to hold my daughter in my arms and what it would finally mean to me when I did.

Chapter Five

OUR FAMILY HEARS

W E WAITED TO have kids for three years, and then I didn't conceive for another three. By then, we were both more than ready. I was hoping for a girl. Throughout my life, I had just always assumed that I'd have a daughter. When I was young, I never dreamt about my wedding day, but I did dream about my daughter.

Tim also wanted to have a daughter; he'd longed to have children. Because of his parents divorcing when he was young, Tim has always wanted to be the kind of hands-on father he had never had. We were both overjoyed when Blake finally entered the world. And we felt the same when Chase followed.

When I became pregnant the third time, I just felt inside that it was another boy. Tim, wanting to be positive, sent me a card that said, "Congratulations, babe, on the birth of our daughter." I knew that the card was an expression of his love, and I really appreciated it, but I just knew that it was wrong. Still, I never prayed for a girl—I didn't believe in messing with fate—I just prayed that I would be happy either way.

When I delivered Austin in August of 2002, I felt joy as I held my little darling tight. I wanted no baby other than him. But I will never forget the look on Tim's face when he saw that brown-haired little boy. I think that for a moment he was afraid that I would be disappointed. But he quickly realized that I was more than just okay. Nevertheless, later that day he said to me, "Let's go to China."

We had talked about adopting a baby girl from China when we first married back in 1991, and I loved that he wanted to continue to expand our family.

Early on in our marriage, Tim would tell me the story of our future deaf daughter, saying that she would look and act exactly like me. "She'll be blonde with two pigtails, wear a red dress and black shoes, and carry a black purse," he'd say, grinning. "And she'll have a strong personality. She'll think that she runs the house! She'll be classy, smart, and stylish." He also said that she'd look just like the Coppertone baby from the television commercial—the little girl who looks back while a cute puppy pulls at her bathing suit, revealing her adorable, little white butt.

I laughed and I believed him, not only because he was describing my reason for being, but also because I was always so blown away by Tim's ability to tell stories—they were always so graphic, visual, and funny. I've always been fascinated by ASL and, in particular, Tim's ASL, how he just paints a picture. It's similar to when a hearing person reads a story to a child and the tone of their voice just captures them. Tim made our future daughter seem so real, so alive, that I could practically reach out and touch her.

When Blake was born in 1997, Tim was beside himself with joy. I was sitting in the hospital bed still exhausted from giving birth, and Tim was sitting in the chair next to me. The nurse did the BAER hearing test to check Blake's hearing right in the room when he was born, and he passed instantly. She jumped for joy, while Tim, my mother, and I just stared at her. Looking back, I think that she had never been in that situation before and realized that she might have made us feel a little uncomfortable because when she left the room, she never came back.

Having a *hearing* child, now that was news. I was thrilled for Blake. I wanted him to have the world at his fingertips. But had he been born deaf, I would have been just fine with it. But I thought that Tim was going to faint—not because he was upset that Blake was hearing but from the shock of it.

For Tim, finding out that his child was hearing was probably just as shocking as when hearing parents find out that their child is deaf. Perhaps it shouldn't have been such a surprise. The genetic counselor we saw when we first started dating told us that we had a 50 percent chance of having hearing children, so Tim knew that there was a definite possibility. Even though he had many hearing friends by then, including some of his best friends, I think that growing up in a family that was so steeped in Deaf Culture and in the Deaf community made the situation impossible for him to even imagine. It just did not compute. And there was little Blake all wrapped up in his hospital blanket, the first hearing child born into his family in well over a century.

For a split second, he wondered how on earth he'd raise a hearing child who would go to public school. He worried how he would communicate with Blake's hearing friends because he wouldn't be able to talk with them. What would happen at Blake's birthday parties since Blake's friends and their parents wouldn't know how to sign? These were all just passing thoughts—gone in a few seconds. After he was over the initial shock, the adjustment felt on par with having to buy blue clothes and trucks instead of pink clothes and dolls. Blake would just have to learn how to sign.

Tim had to make some changes, however, now that we had a hearing child. For example, he had to learn the correct volume for electronics. I remember once before when a few of his hearing friends had come over to watch a baseball game, they told him that he'd turned the volume on the television up so high that it made the entire house shake. Living with deaf people his whole life, he had no reason to be aware of the intricacies of sound. He would turn on the car radio and sort of dance to the beat, only to find out from a hearing friend that he was dancing to a talk show.

When each of the kids was born, we turned on the television for audio stimulation and also played mood music on a boom box to help them fall asleep. My family gave us Beethoven, Mozart, and country music CDs, and told us to turn the volume on the boom box up to five. I, too, needed to be reminded about when I made noise—whether it was turning on the television, closing the cabinets, or with my voice, even—and to be quieter. I had forgotten.

*　*　*

TIM HAD CHARMED me with our deaf daughter story for years. After Blake was born, he stopped telling it. We were just so busy with our lives, and even though each pregnancy brought another opportunity to have a daughter, it wasn't until I was pregnant with Austin, that Tim, being so sure that I was carrying a girl, brought her up again.

Two months after Austin's birth, we registered with Great Wall China Adoption, an international adoption agency in Austin, Texas, where we'd lived for eight years prior to moving to Sioux Falls. Adopting a deaf infant girl seemed impossible, as there aren't any adoption agencies that help you find one. Most deaf babies available for adoption are toddlers, and with three children aged five, three, and one, we thought that an infant would most easily blend in.

We had the perfect plan—we'd go to China when Austin was two, giving us plenty of time to prepare for our fourth child. We would take the trip with my close friend Ann Marie and her husband, Jon. She and I had met back in 1988 at the Miss Deaf America pageant. She was Miss Deaf Minnesota and the first runner-up at the pageant.

The first time I met Ann Marie, I was sitting in a restaurant with Angie and our two chaperones. Ann Marie and her chaperone were sitting in the booth right behind us. We all ended up sitting together and having a great time. Ann Marie was beautiful, tall, and slender with brown, wavy hair. She was oral but signed fluently like me. Years later, after becoming one of my best friends, she was always giving me guff about winning the crown, saying that I'd won because I'd slept with the judges. "Yeah, you're right," I shot back. "I *was* smart enough to do that!"

Ann Marie was very hard of hearing but not profoundly deaf like me, so she was able to hear with hearing aids. Her parents were both hearing like mine, but neither of them had learned how to sign. Her father had quit school early, and her mother had only graduated high school. They sent Ann Marie to hearing schools and didn't expose her to other deaf people. Having no exposure to deafness themselves, they believed that if Ann Marie learned to speak she'd learn to hear. She was very lonely growing up compared to me.

After the Miss Deaf America Pageant, we reconnected the following summer at the YLC, where she was working as a counselor. Then we were in and out of touch for about ten years, connecting mostly through business. In 2003, she moved to Sioux Falls to work at Communication Service for the Deaf (CSD), a nonprofit organization where Tim and I were working that provided communication access to deaf people.

When the ADA was passed in 1990, Title IV of the Act, the part that Tim had worked on while he was working for John McCain, mandated that Telecommunications Relay Services (TRS) (enabling us to use the TTY to communicate with hearing people through the public telephone network) be provided for us. This was a real breakthrough because, as a result, the telephone was finally no longer a barrier for us. TRS put the Deaf community on a much more equal playing field with our hearing counterparts. I had been working for Sprint for eleven years when the company entered the market to establish TRS. At that point, we were able to communicate with hearing people but only by using TTY machines and text.

When video technology came along, it opened up amazing new possibilities for deaf people whose primary language was ASL. CSD, along with other organizations and community leaders, argued that although Title IV of the ADA mandated TTY and its relay services, video technology was a truer representation of the spirit of the law. (The ADA called it "functionally equivalent.") What could be more functionally equivalent than using our own language (ASL) in real time with an interpreter? The Federal Communications Commission agreed, and the Video Relay Services (VRS) industry was born. CSD was the first company to take the risk and invest in developing videophones and the telecommunications services needed for it.

Ann Marie was the company's chief operating officer, and I headed up their marketing department, so we worked closely together. That's when our friendship really blossomed. Serendipitously, she also wanted to adopt a baby girl from China, so we went through the process together.

Our first step was to find a local adoption agency to do our home studies—a process whereby a social worker evaluates you in your home, making sure that you will be fit parents. Both the local and the international adoption agencies would work together so that all things would be in place when it was time to go to China.

We found the New Horizons Adoption Agency, with an office right in Sioux Falls, and signed up with them in April. I filled out enough paperwork to pave a road to China, which made life even more hectic, but all in all, we were doing just fine for a family of five. It was only a matter of time before I would be flying to China to finally bring home my daughter.

A year later in June, when Tim and I were well into the adoption paperwork and processing, we were in Austin one weekend visiting Tim's sister and her kids. I had just come back from a meeting with the folks at Great Wall China Adoption and was telling Tim about it in the parking lot of his sister's apartment complex. Out of the blue, he just looked at me and said, "Brandi, I can't do it. Four kids are too many. I'm sorry."

"What?" I said, trying to breathe.

"We have three wonderful, healthy children," he continued.

"I know. But I want a girl. You said that we could—"

"We hardly see them enough as it is," he replied, cutting me off and becoming more and more upset. "Always dropping them off at day care, being away on business trips all the time. . . . What kind of parents would we be?"

"You're right, I know," I said, "But—"

"No, Brandi. I just can't do it. I'm sorry."

There was no room for discussion. He was adamant, and I knew better than to try to reason with him. I backed off and didn't say anything else. The kids were sitting in the car, and I didn't want to make a scene.

So the summer began with me trying to fix Tim's perception of the situation, believing that if he didn't feel so overwhelmed by having three children, he might be more open to having a fourth. I became supermom, the consummate wife and mother, trying to make life perfect for him by taking on extra responsibilities and lessening his. I got up with the kids, fed and drove them to school and day care, went to work, and then picked them up, drove home, and had dinner waiting on the table for Tim when he came home from work. All he had to do was enjoy the kids before they went to bed. I cleaned the house, did the laundry and food shopping, picked up the dry cleaning, and brought the kids to and from play dates. I did the same thing on weekends. Before that, I'd always asked Tim for help (and he always did his share and never complained). Now, I didn't even ask him.

Doing all of that wasn't even what stressed me out. What stressed me out was the fact that Tim had said no and that my paperwork for China was going to expire in a few months if I didn't complete it. What stressed me out was thinking about how I was going to let go of my longing for a daughter if he didn't change his mind. What really hurt was standing next to someone who had a baby girl— in the store, the doctor's office, at school. I just crumbled inside. I actually felt physical pain. When I went clothes shopping for the boys, I'd trained myself not to look at the girls' section and only pay attention to the boys' clothes.

I was in a desperate state. I even thought about signing Tim's name on the China documents and sending them in without telling him. I'd go to China alone, get the baby, and bring her home. What would he do? Close the door on me? *He wouldn't do that*, I thought. I realized that even if I could pull that off, I didn't want to. I wanted Tim's support and was struggling because I didn't have it.

What made things even more difficult was that I completely identified with Tim's position. I knew how he'd hated telling me no and had struggled to do it. The fact that he was so adamant—even harsh—only showed how his heart was truly aching. When he married me, he knew how much I wanted a daughter. He was in a real predicament with his deep need conflicting so much with mine. He also knew how determined I was, and I think that scared him. I got it. I knew that he was questioning what it meant to be a good parent, knowing that young children like ours needed so much attention.

At one point, before our family moved to Sioux Falls, he lived there without us for three months, traveling back and forth to Austin, where I had remained with the three boys. He did not like that; he had regrets when we were apart. He had always strived to keep his life in balance, going to work, taking care of himself, and also being there for the kids—a senior vice president trying to be a good career man, husband, and father. He was a realist and a family man 100 percent—the most involved father I had ever seen—and he had been from day one. And not because he felt he *had* to but because he *wanted* to be there for his children. He didn't want them to think that he was only thinking of himself. He wanted quality time with them and believed in his gut that it wouldn't be fair to them to add another child to our family.

I loved him more because I understood his reasons. When I told people of my longing for a girl, they looked at me like I was crazy, pointing out that I already had three beautiful and healthy children. I knew that three children were plenty, that Tim and I were incredibly lucky, and that having a fourth child would be insane. But my yearning overrode all of it.

Despite the enormous conflict, it didn't really seem to impact our relationship. Between the kids, work, and traveling, we were both just so busy, there was no time to dwell on it or let resentment fester. Although I was upset, I also truly understood his position and did my best to not let my emotions come between us.

I didn't bring the subject up again until our anniversary, when I thought, *Tonight, I'm going to convince him.* That morning I went out early and bought Tim a newspaper and his favorite coffee from Starbucks. That evening, at Foley's Steak House, I brought the subject up at dinner. He was as firm as ever. I sat there and cried.

The following day, Ann Marie, who knew Tim very well, said to me while I was sitting on her living room couch and still crying, "Brandi, you need to prepare yourself. Tim may never change his mind." Her words made me want to gasp, the way that hearing the truth often does when you're not expecting it. Yet, even though hearing what she said was so difficult, I loved her for saying it, knowing that she was only trying to help and didn't want to see me hurt. Not many people have the ability to sit down with a friend and tell it to them straight with such compassion and understanding. I knew in my heart that I might eventually have to face that truth, but I wasn't there yet. I just thought, *Nope, I'm not going to think about that until the time comes.*

When the last weekend in September rolled around, the pressure was really on because my paperwork for China was going to expire on November 1st. I hadn't mentioned anything to Tim since our anniversary dinner. As a last-ditch attempt, I decided to write him a letter explaining my yearning for a daughter. He was planning on visiting his grandfather in New Jersey, so right before he left for the airport I gave him the letter, asking him to read it on the plane. The Sioux Falls newspaper had written an article on China adoptions a couple weeks before that had a picture of a little Chinese girl with huge, chubby cheeks. I had cut it out and put it on my desk at work. I put the picture in with the letter.

Dear Tim,

I write this letter because all of my recent attempts to convey my desire to have a daughter to you have failed. I only ask that you read it with an open heart and mind. I want you to understand that I love our sons with my entire being. Every day, after waking up in the morning and before going to sleep at night, I have prayed for acceptance that I was meant to only have sons.

I understand how blessed we are to have three healthy, incredible boys. I understand, better than you think, that four children would be too many. We both work full time and want to be there for our children. To add a fourth— ouch—how would we juggle our time and responsibilities? I tell myself to be grateful for what we have—there are so many childless couples out there who desire children, and we have three!

But my need for a daughter is so great that I don't know what else to do other than to continue pursuing that dream. It's like a calling that I must answer. The fact that we did not have a biological daughter only convinces me more that she is out there somewhere—waiting for us to bring her home.

Yet, I cannot pursue this dream without you. I love you, and you are an incredible father. Years ago, you spoke to me of a little girl in a red dress with a black purse and two pigtails. I've seen her in my dreams throughout the years. I ask you to find it in your heart to help me find her and bring her home.

As soon as Tim's plane landed in Newark, he texted me. "Hey, good letter," he said. "Let's discuss when I get home." Sunday evening after he returned home and the boys were in bed, we sat down on the couch and talked. Years later, he said that at the time, he realized he had been too closed-minded about the situation and wanted to be more open. However, looking back, I think that something so much grander had also taken place. I think that Tim's openness was like a signal to the universe. That night in the living room, he told me that even though he still felt that having four children would be too many, we could go ahead and pursue the China adoption. "I cannot deny you your daughter," he said.

The following day, I completed the paperwork for China.

Exactly one week later, on October 4, while pulling out of a friend's driveway, I received an email that changed everything. It was from the New Horizons Adoption Agency.

Hi Brandi!

We have a question for you and Tim. We have a six-month-old baby girl in foster care who has been diagnosed with a severe hearing loss. The birth mother was exposed to someone with chicken pox when she was pregnant and then got a virus called CMV. The baby's brain scan shows that everything is okay there, and there is no syndrome attached to her condition. Would you and Tim like to show a profile to this birth mother for her to consider you for adopting her baby? Please let me know after you and Tim have had a chance to talk about it. We plan to show the birth mother various profiles from prospective adoptive parents and let her choose the adoptive couple. Thanks! Marlys

It was as if the world had stopped turning. As sure as the sun rose and set, I knew that that baby was the daughter I'd been waiting for my whole life. She belonged with me, and I belonged with her. Joy welled up from within, as the knowledge of a divine order more elegant than I'd ever imagined permeated my entire being. Just one week before, Tim had said that he couldn't deny me my daughter. *And there she was*. Had he not said yes, then—or never said no—I might have missed her. It was too perfect!

PART II

The Roads of Others

Chapter Six

JESS AND BJ

L ITTLE DID I know that during that last tumultuous year, starting right around the time when Austin was nine months old and we had just made our adoption plan, somewhere not too far away, several other people had just made their own plans, sealing my and Zoe's fates forever. A young woman felt like a young man had gotten her pregnant, then rejected her, and then wanted to take her baby away.

However, the day that Jess met BJ, she couldn't possibly have known what would come to pass. It was late May. Her day began like any other; she awakened around 7:00 AM, skipped breakfast, and then went to school. Jess was a junior at Fairmont High School, a typical high school for a small Midwestern town like Fairmont, Minnesota, called the City of Lakes, with a population of about 10,000 people. Around 4:00 PM, she went to work at McDonald's, where she had been working for two years, since she was fifteen.

Had anyone asked her, Jess would have said that she hated working at McDonald's, but walking through those golden arches was when her day really began. Her adrenaline started to rush as she and her workmates began discussing all the little dramas of the day. As the only McDonald's for miles around, it was where many of the high school students congregated.

After punching in, she walked over to the drive-up window where she sat for the next four hours taking customers' orders, while her friend sitting three feet away took their money. When there weren't any customers, the two of them gossiped on their headsets. A beautiful girl, something that made her father, Brian, both proud and fearful, Jess had straight, shoulder-length, light brown hair, with blonde streaks—just like all of her friends—that she wore parted to the side.

When BJ entered the restaurant, he immediately caught her eye. He was twenty-two, stood 5'9", and had soft, wavy, brown hair and a medium yet very muscular build. He was wearing a baseball jersey and was with four teammates around his age; they, along with the rest of their team, had driven from Algona, Iowa, an hour north to Fairmont, Minnesota, to play against the town's baseball team.

Minutes later, Jess noticed him and one of his teammates walking back outside and over to the drive-up window where she was sitting. "I'd like a glass of water, please," he said to her, grinning. Smiling coyly, she gave him one and then, as if right on cue, began bantering with him, speaking in that secret language of flirting teenagers. However, as the number of cars in the drive-up line grew, she quickly scribbled her phone number down on a folded napkin and they said good-bye.

Jess and BJ talked on the phone throughout the entire month of June for hours at a time, and Jess found that she adored BJ's laid back, easygoing manner. One day he said to her, "Just come see me. It's time we got together." A few months later, Jess would say, "He sweet-talked me into driving down by making me feel all guilty," but at the time she was game, thinking how cool it would be to have an older boyfriend. She made plans to spend July 4th evening with him.

Used to lying to her father, she had no problem concocting a story about where she was going, telling him that she was staying at a friend's house and then giving him a bogus girl's name. Since moving back in with him after living with her mother during her freshman year, she told him one lie after another without batting an eyelash. Her mother was much more lenient, and she didn't want him messing up her hallowed plans.

Her parents had gotten divorced when she was six— oh, how Jess hated being shuffled back and forth between them—and as she got older, she struggled to understand what love really meant. Her father had dated several women after he and her mother split, but he never committed to anyone. Perhaps that was the reason Jess didn't trust guys all that much and tended to form superficial relationships. She knew from firsthand experience that people tended to disappear.

As with a lot of teenage girls, her social skills were her strength, and nothing was more important than her friends. School ranked low on the totem pole of importance. Jess never did her homework, and her grades were tumbling. She cut school during the day and snuck out of the house at night; either a friend would pick her up or she would take her own car. At one point, her father even took away her car keys; however, she had a spare set and would sneak out of the house after he went to bed. This was a vicious cycle, with each lie covering up the one that came before, until even Jess felt like her life was one big lie.

Jess's father tried reasoning with her, but chatting on the Internet and talking on her cell phone, along with the other things she was doing, were just too big a draw for his rules to have any impact. They established an uneasy relationship—she lied, which upset and angered him, and then he yelled and punished her. This saddened her father greatly. He missed their camaraderie; when she was younger, they had been great pals. But Jess had built up so much resentment toward him that she even made her father out to be horrible to her friends.

Still she always tried to do the right thing. Once, when she had been drinking at a party, instead of driving home, she got a lift and asked a friend of hers to drive her car home for her. She waited nervously for the sound of her car engine in the driveway. After twenty minutes had passed, she called her friend, who informed her that she had gotten into a car accident; she had dropped a cigarette while driving and decided to search for it. "You got what? You did what?" Jess screamed into the phone. At 2:00 AM, she had had to wake up her father, who was asleep on the couch; he was very angry, and Jess was really scared this time.

They went to the crash site only to discover that her friend had rolled the car—it had hit the curb, rolling over twice, and had landed in a ditch; it was totaled. Fortunately, no one was hurt. The police gave Jess a Breathalyzer test, probably because it was her car that had been wrecked. Her father stood there watching. She blew a .01, which wasn't above the legal limit for driving, but she got a ticket for being a minor drinking underage. Her father made her pay for both the ticket and the month-long chemical awareness program she had to take, and the incident also cost Jess her spot on the school softball team. This really upset her because she just loved cracking that ball. She'd started playing softball when she was eleven, usually playing second base, and she was an outstanding batter.

On July 4th, after giving her father the phony friend's name, she turned off her cell phone, and with two six-packs in her trunk, hit the road with a friend. Three hours later, at 7:00 PM, they arrived in Algona and met BJ and one of his friends in the parking lot of the tournament field. BJ was in his uniform, all grubby and sweaty from playing six hours of baseball, but looking as cute as ever. The parking lot was packed with cars and people who were just hanging around and having a good time while waiting for the fireworks to begin.

They chatted for a while, and then Jess and her friend accompanied BJ back to his house and waited for him to take a shower. Soon after, BJ's friend arrived, and the four of them piled into BJ's truck, along with Jess's beer. She was really excited, very attracted to BJ, and loving the idea of being with an older guy. The four of them drove around for a while, laughing, drinking beer, having a great time, and then headed for a cabin in the woods that belonged to the parents of one of BJ's friends. When they reached the cabin, they'd already polished off the two six-packs, so they drank some vodka that they'd found there. Well, one thing led to another and before Jess knew it, she was very drunk and in bed having sex with BJ.

Driving home the following morning, Jess felt pretty awful about the whole thing, and the five voicemails waiting for her from her father didn't help. "Where the hell are you, girl?" he shouted, each time louder than the time before. Five weeks later, after missing her period, Jess took two home pregnancy tests that both turned out positive. (She carefully threw the sticks and wrappers away, so that her father wouldn't find them.) Yet, even though she had been terrified for weeks that she was pregnant, she thought for sure the tests were false positives. Still, just to be sure, she asked her friend Ashley to go with her to Planned Parenthood, which was located about an hour away in Mankato.

At 10:00 AM, the following morning, they pulled into the parking lot of a yellow, three-story building and went inside. Nervously, Jess told the receptionist why she was there, and then sat down and filled out the forms that the woman had given her. Ten minutes later, an overweight nurse with a big smile on her face greeted her and took her to the lab to draw blood. After that, Jess sat in the waiting room until the nurse returned fifteen minutes later with her test results.

"Jess," she said, this time with a tentative smile. Jess looked up at her, shaking.

"I'm so sorry, hon, but your blood test came back positive. You're pregnant and . . ."

The rest of what she said faded out completely, until Jess heard the words, "due date" and "March 26," when her heart stopped and her stomach fell while the words reverberated in her head. She felt as though there was nothing to grab onto and no floor beneath her feet. She burst into tears—the reality of the situation killing her inside. Her first thought was that her father was going to kill her; rebel that she was, Jess still couldn't stand disappointing him like this.

After giving her a moment to recover, the nurse continued, "I know that it's a shock, but it's going to be all right. Do you have any family or friends who can help you to decide what you want to do?"

At first, Jess didn't respond and then shook her head no. The nurse opened a folder she had and gave her some booklets and brochures to read.

"Let's talk about your options, which are to have an abortion or to raise the baby," she continued, mentioning nothing about adoption. Years later, Jess remembered that conversation, thinking how ridiculous it was that at Planned Parenthood, of all places, she wasn't told about adoption. She herself would later stand before a class of high school students, telling them all about Zoe and about her positive experience with choosing to place her for adoption. However, at the time, she didn't even notice the omission, not knowing anything about the process herself.

"Do you know what you want to do?" the nurse went on. Jess shook her head no. For a split second, she'd considered having an abortion, but quickly dismissed it because abortion went against her strict Lutheran upbringing.

She stumbled out of the clinic and called her mother, who immediately uttered, "Oh my God. Maybe you'll have a miscarriage." A woman of forty-six, her heart ached as she felt her daughter's shock, devastation, and turmoil. She remembered Jess telling her just a few weeks before, almost desperately, that she had started taking the pill, and realized that when Jess had told her that, she must have already known that she was pregnant and was hoping that taking it would make her "unpregnant" or knock the baby out, or something—which was exactly what Jess was hoping. When her mother first heard Jess talk about BJ, she had been very troubled by the fact that he was older than Jess, thinking about all of the liquor he could buy, and how Jess, at seventeen, was at such a different stage of life than the twenty-two-year-old young man.

Working in human services determining welfare eligibility for single mothers, Jess's mother, Sonia, saw what those young women went through, during their pregnancies and afterward, and she had always prayed that Jess would never find herself in that situation. However, quickly putting her thoughts and feelings aside and finding her center, she assured Jess that together they would figure out what the best thing was for her to do.

After talking with her mother, Jess and Ashley drove to Ashley's grandmother's house, where Ashley was living. She got lost, knowing which direction she needed to go but not the exact roads. On the way there, she anxiously smoked a half a pack of cigarettes, the last cigarettes that she smoked throughout her entire pregnancy.

Eventually they arrived, and Ashley's grandmother, at sixty-four, was very understanding of Jess's situation and was warm and compassionate. However, she insisted that Jess call her father to tell him what had happened. Sitting at the woman's kitchen table, Jess dialed her father's phone number, bracing herself. When he answered the phone, she paused for a second then said, "Dad, hi."

Silence.

"Dad, are you there? I have to tell you something."

"Where are you?" he fumed, upset because she had told him she would be home by now.

"I'm at Ashley's grandma's house. I'm pregnant," she blurted out. He didn't hear what she said and asked her to repeat it.

"I got pregnant," she said again, starting to cry.

"What? You idiot. How could you be so stupid?" he shouted. "Your life is ruined. All my hopes and dreams for you are gone."

Except for dying, Jess's father thought that becoming pregnant was the worst fate that could ever happen to an unmarried female child. "You'd better not come home tonight," he continued.

At that point, Jess threw her cell phone down on the floor, sobbing, and Ashley's grandmother picked it up and started talking to Jess's father, trying to console him. When Jess got home the following morning, he did allow her into the house but didn't talk to her the whole day.

A few days later, while driving on his truck route (he delivered parts for an electrical company), he pulled over and called Jess, giving her an ultimatum. "Jess, you cannot lie to me anymore," he said. "The lies are done. From now on, you have to be 100 percent honest with me. Do you hear what I am saying?"

"Okay, Dad," she said, his words going in one ear and out the other, as always.

But that evening, Jess had an epiphany.

Her father, who had often turned to God when he was in a spiritual quandary, had asked their pastor to come over to give them his support. The pastor arrived at 7:00 PM, and as the three of them walked into the living room, he smiled at Jess and then thanked them both for inviting him to come over. Although Jess didn't know the pastor personally, she had always been drawn to him at church because of his respectful, kind, and nonjudgmental manner and his thoughtful sermons. He had always put her at ease.

That night she felt drawn to him more than ever before, as they sat in her father's living room, he on the rocking chair, her father on the leather couch, and Jess on the love-seat, all cuddled up in a blanket.

"How are you doing, Jess?" he asked her, settling into the rocking chair.

"Oh, all right," Jess said softly, wrapping the blanket around her more tightly.

"You may think that I'm here to tell you about 'rights' and 'wrongs,'" he continued, leaning in toward her slightly, "however, I'm not. Your father has told me that you already feel bad enough."

Jess closed her eyes.

"What's done is done," he continued. "It's water under the bridge. Just remember, Jess, that whatever you do in this life, whether it is right or wrong, God is always with you."

"I know," Jess said, glancing over at her father.

Then the pastor said, "What is important now are the decisions that you make moving forward."

As Jess listened to the pastor's words and felt his calm, soothing voice and kind manner, her heart began opening. His acceptance of her made her trust him even more.

"At a difficult time like this," he went on, "what will pull you through is finding the love that is inside your heart—the love that you have for your baby, your father and mother, and also for yourself."

Jess's father cleared his throat.

"Most importantly," the pastor went on, "you need to be honest, Jess. Now, more than ever, you need to be honest with your father, and especially with yourself."

That was the turning point.

Now the truth for Jess was no longer lurking some-where below her conscious level but was as evident as if she were seeing it face-to-face on a summer's day. *Oh, my gosh. I need to be honest,* she thought. *I'm not going to get very far continuing to lie.* Her heart had opened, just like that. The pastor had finally gotten through to her just like Father Tom had finally gotten through to me.

"Thank you," Jess said to the pastor. "Thank you so much." She smiled at her father, a huge weight lifting from her shoulders, as "Jess, the liar" dissolved into thin air and "Jess, the responsible mother and young woman" was born. She finally realized that it was not a sign of weak-ness but a sign of strength to share with others and reach out and ask for help—and that she needed her parents' help then more than ever. She also realized that if she had respected herself more that night in the cabin with BJ, she wouldn't have gotten drunk and gone to bed with him. But what the pastor had said was right: what's done is done. She would have more self-respect from that moment on.

After that night, Jess was honest with her father about whom she was with and where she was going and always came home on time. It took a little while, but eventually their relationship began to heal, and they became a real team. Her father strongly believed that Jess should place her baby for adoption. He knew how much she wanted go to college, and if she raised the baby, it would dash those plans and cause her to go on welfare. He believed that adoption was the best thing for both Jess and her baby. But Jess wasn't so sure; she didn't know anything about adoption.

The pastor had recommended that she go to the Caring Pregnancy Center, a nonprofit organization in Fairmont where pregnant teenagers can go to get answers. She would go the following day. But first she called BJ, whom she hadn't heard from since they'd spent the night together. He immediately wanted to come and see her, so they arranged to meet at Gomsrud Park, a student stomping ground where Jess often hung out. Too afraid to be alone with him because of her vulnerable state, she asked her friends to come with her.

* * *

WHEN BJ RECEIVED Jess's call, the whistle was just about to blow at the construction site where he was working. At first he didn't know what to say, thinking that the baby might not be his. But when Jess told him that she hadn't been with anyone else, he believed her.

It was funny. He believed that the baby was his, but there was something more to it than that. While he felt like an idiot for getting Jess pregnant, he seemed almost proud that he was going to be a father. Even as a small boy, he believed that having a child was the most precious thing in life, the one thing that was completely yours and that nobody else could take away from you. He felt that nobody else's opinion mattered when it came to having a child. When he heard that he was going to be a father, his paternal instincts awakened. He felt a rightness about the whole situation.

As soon as he heard that Jess was pregnant with his baby, he drove right up to see her, hoping to begin a real relationship with her. He wanted to start spending time with her, to take her out for dinner, and go for walks in the park. In fact, when he arrived at Gomsrud Park and saw that her friends were with her, his heart sank; he wanted to be alone with her, so that they could really talk.

What a weird encounter it must have been: a young father-to-be sitting on a park bench next to the mother of his child, whom four months earlier he hadn't even known existed—and who now acted like she didn't have the time of day for him. During the five hours that they were together, her friends were there practically the whole time. He could tell that she didn't want to be alone with him, and somewhere inside he sort of understood, even if he felt bad about it. He had gone to bed with her and then hadn't even called her.

But his heart was in the right place.

When they were finally alone, BJ sat down on a park bench next to Jess and asked her, "Do you know what you want to do about the baby?"

"No," Jess responded. "But I'm thinking about adoption. My due date is March 26."

BJ's heart skipped a beat. "Wow. When you told me the news, I was kind of hoping that you would keep the baby and that we'd both raise it," he said, trying to sound hopeful. "We don't have to get married or anything," he continued, "but maybe we can live near each other and raise the baby together."

Jess smiled but didn't respond. She looked very pretty to him in her white jeans, Doc Marten sandals, and dark blue Hollister shirt.

After a moment of awkward silence, BJ went on, "I'm glad that you don't want to have an abortion. Personally, I'm neither for nor against them." He continued, "If I were a woman, I wouldn't choose to have an abortion, but I wouldn't hold it against any woman who did."

"I don't really believe in abortion," Jess responded. "It goes against my religion, although many of my friends would have one." She stared at the sky for a few seconds and then said, "I either want to raise the baby or place it for adoption."

"I don't have anything against adoption," BJ shot back. "My brother adopted a kid, and my little nephew is totally awesome."

"I have a feeling that it's going to be a girl," Jess said, looking at her belly. "I can just tell."

"Well, I'll bet you're right. Do you know what you want to name her?" BJ asked, brushing a piece of lint off his shirt.

"Well, actually, I was kind of thinking about calling her *Emma*."

"*Emma's* a cool name," said BJ. "I've always liked the name *Grace*."

"Maybe we'll call her *Emma Grace*," Jess replied.

BJ liked the name *Emma Grace*, but what he liked even more was picking the name out with Jess. It was the first thing they did for their child together. He wanted involvement from the very start; he craved it. He wanted to go through Jess's pregnancy with her, to watch his baby grow, and know how the baby and Jess were doing. He wanted to go to the obstetrician with Jess, be there during her ultrasounds, and help her make decisions. He knew that things wouldn't be easy but was thinking that if they could work things out between them, they might eventually even get married.

Jess said that she had a headache and asked BJ if he would drive to Shopko with her to get some aspirin. They got into Jess's car, a 1992 gray Cutlass Ciera with red interior, Jess behind the wheel and BJ in the passenger seat. Pictures of Jess and her friends were pinned to the lining of the roof and taped to the dashboard. BJ felt really awkward and nervous being in such close quarters with her. He didn't know what to do or what to say. But acting in good faith, he took a chance and leaned over and tried to kiss her, thinking that it might be a good way to begin their relationship.

Jess immediately recoiled, and then BJ also retreated, back into the awkward silence.

After getting the aspirin, it was already quite late, and Jess said that she had to go home. They said good-bye, and BJ drove home confused, wondering when he would see her again. He didn't know that his attempted kiss, something he hoped would bond the two of them together, would deprive him of the very thing for which he craved: to be involved in her pregnancy. Jess wouldn't see him or return his phone calls for a long time.

BJ's father, a warm-hearted police officer named Dale, was quite dismayed when BJ told him the news. It was Saturday morning. BJ had come downstairs to the kitchen. His father was sitting at the kitchen table reading the newspaper, and his mother, Joann, was at the stove cooking some omelets and bacon. The coffee was brewing. BJ walked over to the counter, poured himself a glass of orange juice, drank it, and then sat down at the kitchen table. "There's something I have to tell you guys," he said, slapping his thighs, immediately letting his parents know that something wasn't right.

"What is it?" his mother said, looking straight at him.

He paused for a few seconds then blurted out, "Well . . . I kind of got a girl pregnant."

His mother almost dropped the frying pan. "Oh, no," she yelped, immediately thinking about a good friend of his who had been in a similar situation—a real mess. She continued, "Are you sure that the baby is—"

"Yeah, it's mine," BJ said, interrupting her before she had a chance to finish. "Remember I told you about a girl, Jess . . . she's from Fairmont . . . we got together after the tournament . . . and one thing led to another and—"

"Was there any drinking involved?" his father asked, interrupting him.

BJ nodded.

For several seconds no one said anything, and then his father continued, while shaking his head in disapproval, "Well, I don't have to tell you how disappointed we are in you, BJ. You should know better."

"I know, Dad. But come on. It wasn't only my fault," BJ shot back, a little defensively.

"I'm not interested in what this gal did or didn't do. I'm interested in you," his father replied, sounding a bit exasperated.

BJ's father was a well-grounded, even-tempered man, who had recently retired from the police force and was working as the community coordinator for Kasson County, Iowa. While on the force, he had been involved with a lot of domestic-type situations—teenage parents trying to deal with their messed up lives with their babies stuck in the middle. BJ's mother, an obstetrics nurse, had done well-baby checkups over the years, caring for infants who were being placed for adoption. A foster mother used to bring her babies to the clinic in Algona where she worked and would tell her things about them, like where their birth parents lived and how old they were.

"Well, at any rate, you should take a paternity test," his mother said, to which BJ didn't respond.

Then after a short pause, he said, "Jess is considering placing the baby for adoption, but I'm hoping that she'll keep it. I'm hoping that we can work things out and raise her together. She thinks she's having a girl."

His parents were both quiet. A million things were going through their minds. As a cop and a nurse, both had been around teenage pregnancies, and neither had ever heard of any custody battles working out. They were also disturbed that he didn't seem interested in taking a paternity test.

But knowing Jess's due date and doing the math, he felt certain that the baby was his. It was almost as if he didn't want to take the test because he had already made up his mind.

Even though BJ knew that his parents were disappointed in him, he also knew that they loved him and would be there for him, just like they had been his entire life. They were a very close-knit family. BJ's parents had always supported their children, helping them through the difficult times, like the time a few years earlier when BJ's older brother and his wife lost their twin infants. His brother's wife had gone into premature labor when she was seven-and-a-half-months pregnant. When his mother received the phone call about it, BJ was in school, so she arranged for him to go to a friend's house, and then she, his father, and his sister drove four hours to the hospital to be with BJ's brother, his brother's wife, and the dying babies.

The five of them sat there rocking the babies, who had been put on respirators, and then BJ's brother and his brother's wife rocked them gently until they died. One gasped and then the other. Oh, how it hurt BJ's mother so that the only thing she could ever do for those babies was to pick them up and drive them to the funeral home in Algona. BJ's brother had wanted BJ to see them; he wanted him to say good-bye, so the following day the two of them went to the funeral home and just sat there for a few hours and held them and talked. The funeral director said that it was the most touching thing that he had ever seen in his entire life. BJ was the pallbearer at the funeral. All by himself, he carried the casket with those babies in it.

BJ's parents, after getting over their initial shock and disappointment, told him that whether he wanted to support Jess with an adoption plan or raise the baby, they would be there for him. They felt that even though they weren't getting any younger (he was forty-eight and she was forty-six), if BJ wanted to raise the baby, they would step up to the challenge and do whatever they had to do to support their son.

* * *

MEANWHILE, JESS WENT to the Caring Pregnancy Center, which was true to its name. Even though she was extremely nervous when she first arrived, the center's bright and cheery atmosphere, with children's books and copies of *Parents* magazine strewn all around, put her at ease. One of the center's owners, a warm and caring woman named Janet, whom Jess confided in for months to come, came to greet her. Janet then showed her around the center, taking her first to a big room that had maternity clothes, baby clothes, and toys that their clients could take, as needed. After that she took her to a video room, where Jess would watch many videos and fill out workbooks, and where she and Janet would have many long talks about the effects of pregnancy on her body and about her three different options for moving forward. It was here at the Caring Pregnancy Center that Jess was introduced to adoption. At first, she was so relieved just knowing that raising her baby or having an abortion weren't her only options because neither of them had felt right to her from the very start. Adoption really intrigued Jess, and she knew that it was her father's choice; yet she knew nothing about it at all. A while back, a friend of hers had placed her baby for adoption, so she knew that people did such a thing, but she didn't have a clue as to why or how.

In the past, when she had thought of the word "adoption," she conjured up images of orphans in dreary orphanages with mean caretakers, who were lucky enough to get picked by some benevolent couple and "get adopted" like the character in *Annie*. She also thought that if she placed her baby for adoption, people would look down on her and think she was being selfish. When she told an adopted friend of hers that she was considering adoption for her baby, her friend said, "*I* could never give up *my* baby because I would love it too much," obviously speaking much more about her own unresolved life experiences and unable to see the situation from Jess's perspective.

Jess had certainly never thought about adoption from a *birth mother's* point of view. The whole idea of giving her baby to someone else felt so weird and uncomfortable; yet, the more she learned about adoption, the more she wanted to know. Eventually, she began thinking that it might actually be the light at the end of the tunnel. Because of her interest, Janet referred her to the New Horizons Adoption Agency, whose main office was in Frost, Minnesota, not too far from her home. She called them immediately and arranged to meet with their director, Marlys, at the Perkins Restaurant in town one afternoon after school.

Marlys reminded Jess of Mrs. Doubtfire when they first met. It wasn't so much her clothes, but her big glasses, gray hair (minus the bun), and her very warm and kind eyes. She looked very tall, sitting there, in her grayish trousers and cream-colored, buttoned-up blouse with a bow that you tie at the neck. She was sipping a cup of chicken soup.

"You must be Jess. It's very nice to meet you," Marlys said, looking straight at her.

"Hi. It's great to meet you, too," Jess replied, meeting her gaze and then looking away.

Marlys smiled and then continued, "Well, the eats are very good here. Would you care to order something?"

"Oh, thank you, but I'm not all that hungry right now," Jess replied, but still picked up the menu, skimmed it, and then decided to order a bowl of minestrone soup. She felt shy that first day, but from then on, she ordered enormous amounts of food—a big burger with fries or an ice cream sundae or a milkshake, whatever she was craving. She ate like a horse, while Marlys always had her cup of chicken soup.

And so a relationship began that anchored and sustained Jess during the most tumultuous time of her entire life. Over the next several months, Marlys told her everything there was to know about domestic adoption. She learned about how she would choose an adoptive family; about open, semi-open, and closed adoptions; and how birth parents and adoptive parents meet and, through the adoption agency, work out an arrangement. She heard stories about birth mothers who had successfully placed their babies with an adoptive family and about those few who had eventually decided to raise their child on their own. Marlys always stressed that there was no "right" or "wrong," but that every birth mother had to decide what was right for her own life. Jess's parents met with Marlys a few times, as well, and they were very onboard with Jess's inquiry.

Marlys had been there and done this dance with scores of birth mothers over the years, yet never made Jess feel like she had to be different from who she was. That's what Jess loved about her the most. Without judgment, she encouraged Jess to experience her emotions as they came. She never pushed Jess toward adoption, but she gave her good information so that she could make up her own mind. Marlys prepared Jess for what she would experience down the road, explaining that on some days she would feel perfectly fine and others like a complete mess.

She seemed to know exactly what Jess was thinking and feeling and could tell when she was having an "off" day, which Jess really appreciated because her emotions and her hormones were raging. Marlys listened as Jess told her about school, her parents, her friends, and her changing body. She told Marlys about her desire to have a successful career, be married, and have children someday, and about her mixed feelings toward BJ, which would become more difficult for her to deal with as the months progressed. Marlys was like Jess's guide, and Jess felt like she would have died without her.

Little by little, the shock of being pregnant faded into the reality of Jess caring for herself and her unborn baby. Even though her life was in enormous upheaval, she was still in absolute awe of the miracle that was taking place inside of her. She saw her baby as an extension of herself, and her love for the baby expanded into her having more self-love and self-respect. As a result, she found herself cleaning her room, taking other people's feelings into consideration—especially her father's—doing her home-work, and going to bed early. She ate three balanced meals a day with her priority being her baby's health and also her own health—physical and emotional. She didn't even mind losing most of her friends, who couldn't at all relate to what she was going through and weren't all that inter-ested. She knew that what she needed most was to find clarity about what she truly wanted from life and about what would be best for her baby—the latter becoming nothing short of her life's mission.

Yet the answer to that question was still far from being answered. At first, even though placing her baby for adop-tion sounded good in theory, it was still too painful for Jess to even think about not raising the baby—to let go of that idea. But her other alternative was just as painful because she believed that a pregnant woman should be married and planning joyously for her baby's arrival and for motherhood. Oh, how she wished to God that she were that person.

Then there was BJ to contend with, whose kiss she had misinterpreted to mean that he only wanted her sexually and not emotionally. She'd remembered her mother saying to her when she told her that she had met him, that the only thing a twenty-two-year-old guy ever wanted from a seventeen-year-old girl was sex. Desperately needing her mother's support, she didn't have the wherewithal to question her line of thinking. She wasn't able to see that BJ wanted to have a relationship with her after she became pregnant.

She was so unsure about what she wanted to do about the baby, and in such turmoil, she couldn't even begin to consider the fact that BJ would have any feelings on the matter whatsoever, let alone be open to considering them. She was just so scared and confused, and just trying to make it through the day, while her life was falling apart around her.

She felt selfish for wanting to place her baby for adoption, but also selfless, knowing that if she did, the baby would have a much better life. And she couldn't even begin to think about raising the baby with BJ. A long time ago, she'd decided that no child of hers would ever be shuffled back and forth between its parents like she had been.

Then there was her lifelong dream of going to college, graduating with a degree, and having a successful career. If she kept her baby, college would be out of the question, at least for the foreseeable future. And she had already been accepted at South Dakota State. Through the grapevine, she had heard about single mothers in town on welfare who were dealing with custody battles and looking for work, who couldn't find anything better than a clerk position at a gas station—*and, by God, she didn't want to be that person*. She'd wanted out of Fairmont—bad—and had seen too many townies over the years grow up and never leave, and that thought was revolting to her. She wanted to make her parents proud and make herself proud. She believed that she deserved that, no matter what her sins.

After much resistance, Jess's father finally convinced her to let BJ know what she was thinking. A meeting was arranged with Jess, BJ, their parents, and Jess's pastor at Jess's father's house, where things became even more entangled.

Chapter Seven

LOVE'S SACRIFICE

E VEN THOUGH BJ's parents said that they would support him if he decided to raise the baby, given the circumstances, his father strongly believed that placing the baby for adoption would be best. His mother did too, yet deep down, part of her would also have been very happy with the alternative. With her three kids all grown, there was something very appealing to her about having a little baby—*her grandchild*—crawling around the house. To her, family was everything.

His parents were right by his side from the very start, attending the first meeting with Jess's pastor and then several others, some of which were incredibly difficult. However, they made it very clear to BJ that it was *his* situation and not theirs, and that he had to decide what he wanted to do.

The pastor looked at them and said, "In God's eyes, the baby must not be aborted." It was a Sunday and still warm the day they drove up to Jess's house for the meeting. When BJ received the phone call from Jess's father inviting them to come, he was really psyched, hoping that he and Jess could finally talk. There was so much he wanted to get out in the open. BJ and his parents, along with Jess and her parents, all sat in the living room listening attentively.

"I understand that you went to the Caring Pregnancy Center, Jess," the pastor said. "Did you find it helpful?"

"I think so," she replied, looking down.

"Have you gained any clarity about what you want to do?"

"Well, I'm not positive," she said nervously, "but I'm thinking about placing the baby for adoption."

BJ closed his eyes and sank back in the loveseat.

The pastor leaned in toward him and said, "How about you, my son? What are your feelings on the matter?"

BJ sat up straight and then said, "Well, I guess I was thinking about raising the baby . . . with Jess . . . or if she doesn't want to be involved . . . by myself."

"It's a big decision," his mother interjected, "and perhaps adoption *is* the best choice." She looked at her husband and continued. "However, we told BJ that if he wants to raise the baby and can work things out with Jess, we will help him in any way we can."

Jess's parents coiled back in their seats. From the very start, her mother's protective instincts were on fire. She seemed to be biting her tongue, as if she were ready to lay into BJ, ready to blame him for the whole situation. Because of BJ's reticence, and the fact that he was still living with his parents at twenty-two, Jess's parents both thought that his parents were pushing him to raise the baby because *they* wanted to raise it, and not him. Perhaps they picked up on his mother's mixed emotions.

The meeting was more for the parents, anyway. After Jess and BJ both said their piece, they took a backseat to them. Their parents, of course, were only trying to do the right thing for their children. It was a tough situation: BJ wanted to parent, and Jess wanted adoption. This predicament would be challenging for two mature adults who had been married for years and were the best of friends, let alone two young people, seventeen and twenty-two, who barely knew each other and whose parents had their own agendas.

"It would be very difficult for Jess to raise the baby," Jess's father interjected. "She's not at a point in her life where she can take care of a child on her own." He glanced over at his ex-wife and then added, "Her mother and I are divorced, and I'm not looking to raise a grandchild in my house at this time."

"It's a very complicated situation," the pastor said. "We need to consider everyone's needs, but most importantly the baby's."

"That's exactly what I'm trying to do . . ." Jess blurted out, ". . . think about the baby."

"Jess is an athlete," her mother chimed in, trying to build up her daughter's case. "Now, her high school athletic career is ruined."

BJ's mother could feel her disappointment, knowing how much BJ had also loved participating in school sports, and knowing how much she'd have hated to see him give up something he loved. She felt for Jess's father, too, who seemed like a nice guy, just trying to clean up the mess he had with his teenage daughter.

Most of all, her heart went out to Jess, who appeared to be a very sweet girl who, unfortunately, had gotten in a mess with her son. BJ's father felt the same way. They both wondered if she and BJ might be able to work things out, but clearly understood why Jess didn't feel prepared to raise the baby and respected—even admired—her for it.

"We think that the best thing for everyone concerned is placing the baby for adoption," Jess's father finally said.

BJ, still trying to relax in the loveseat, hadn't said another word. While he could see why Jess's parents were angry with him, he still felt awful about it. He wished the conversation would focus more on his and Jess's relationship. He longed to know what was in her heart and on her mind, and he wanted to share his feelings with her because he truly cared about her and because he thought it would help him to be with his baby.

The fact was that Jess *would* have had a relationship with him if only he had told her that he wanted one. But they were like star-crossed lovers, and the situation was taking on a life of its own. Clearly, other forces were at play.

Two weeks later, the discussion continued for them and their parents at Perkins. Jess had wanted BJ to learn about adoption, so a meeting with Marlys was arranged.

"The New Horizons Adoption Agency has had great success with placing babies for adoption," Marlys said in a friendly, neutral manner. "We help birth parents and adoptive families find suitable matches."

Marlys continued, "In a closed adoption, the adoptive parents and the birth parents have no contact after the placement is made. In a semi-open adoption, the adoptive parents send the birth parents annual updates about the child, via the adoption agency. In an open adoption, the adoptive parents and the birth parents work out their own arrangement."

BJ listened. However, it was very hard for him to take in what Marlys was saying because he could tell that from the moment she laid eyes on him she didn't like him. Sure, she smiled and was friendly. However, the way she seemed to just stare right through him made him wonder if, just like Jess's parents, she blamed him entirely for what had happened and for trying to hurt Jess.

While he just sat there and let his parents do most of the talking, he was thinking, *Stop casting me aside. You need to know that if my child were with me, in my world, surrounded by all the wonderful people who love me, she would have everything she ever needs.* Unlike his parents, BJ knew single mothers and fathers whom, he believed, were very good parents. He was even friendly with their kids and appreciated that it wasn't easy for them not having a mother or father around. But he honestly believed that they were happy and thriving.

Financially, he believed he could swing it. Between construction and landscaping, the jobs had been plentiful, and he believed that he could get extra work, if he needed it, as well. His father had already talked to him about money and the practical side of things, and he listened. BJ always listened whenever his parents talked to him, and he loved hearing their perspective, but some things in life he just had to figure out on his own so that he could live with himself later on.

He pictured buying a small house, near his parents' house. While he was working, his parents, brother, and sister would help take care of the child; they'd already told him they would—and he knew that they were that kind of family. He reminded himself that his parents had already raised three children, and his brother was raising two.

"You're going to be carting this child back and forth, the two of you ending up hating each other," Jess's father continued. He was so angry at BJ—he even thought about suing him for statutory rape, even though he didn't have a case. Marlys, thank goodness, helped him to come to his senses.

"Well, I hope that you'll at least think about adoption, BJ," Marlys finally said.

The meeting ended without bringing them any closer to a resolution.

As the weeks passed, BJ's resentment and anxiety grew. He just couldn't understand why Jess was still keeping him in the dark about his own baby. He didn't know that there was a veil between them. He continued calling her, still hoping to talk things out. Then when he didn't reach her, he became afraid that something terrible had happened—to both her and the baby. The *not knowing* was killing him. The more that she ignored him, the more he needed to be heard and the more he felt victimized and as if he had no control of the situation.

Like always, he turned to his family—his parents, and of course his brother, who because of his trials with his own children, was particularly sensitive to BJ's situation. He also had an incredibly strong bond with his sister; either they were fighting fiercely, or they were the best of friends. Only a year apart in age, she was like a second mother to him and got away with saying things that nobody else could ever say to him. When BJ had introduced her to Jess on the night of the tournament, she did *not* have a good feeling about it. She even asked him, "BJ, what are you thinking?" Later on, when the whole story came out, she came down hard on him, saying that he shouldn't have slept with someone so young, and that for goodness sakes, he should have used some protection.

He also had his friends. When they went out for a few drinks, BJ unloaded all of his anguish and frustrations about being out of the loop and about the possibility of never being able to meet his own child. He questioned if he was being selfish by wanting to be with Jess, but didn't think that he was. But he also felt that what he wanted would probably never happen, as if somehow he had always known the inevitable. He talked about his depression, and he cried.

From the very start, BJ did understand why Jess was pushing for adoption. He appreciated that it was *her* body—that *she* was the one who was pregnant, and the

one who would soon give birth, and that if she relinquished her child, she might feel like she was giving up a
big part of herself. Despite all of that, BJ believed that his
child belonged with him.

* * *

BACK AT FAIRMONT High School, Jess's predicament spread
like wildfire; the first day back from summer vacation, she
was the talk of the school. The die was cast the moment
she called the school's gossip queen while driving home
from Planned Parenthood. She couldn't even walk down
the halls without girls calling her "slut" or "whore." Every
time she turned around, she heard them whispering about
her behind her back. Then the next day, those same girls
came over to her all excited, asking if they could feel her
belly. It made her nauseated.

The school was incredibly cliquey, and Jess had been
in the "popular" clique. During free periods, they all hung
around by the lockers and in the cafeteria, and after school
at Gomsrud Park, where Jess had met with BJ. But now,
feeling ostracized, she threw herself into her schoolwork
and went from class to class, hardly talking to anyone. She
lost a lot of friends. On some mornings, she practically
had to force herself to go to school because she didn't want
to face *the girls*. She felt like a lone soldier out there.

Thank goodness for her "Circle of Trust," the four
friends she hung out with during last period each day,
when seniors could do whatever they wanted. The five of

them met by the locker area and then sat around eating Peanut M&Ms and drinking Dr. Pepper while telling each other their secrets and stories. Over the months, they'd take pictures of Jess's belly, noticing how much it had grown.

Jess told it to them straight: "I gained another three pounds. I felt the baby kick. I had my ultrasound. It's definitely a girl."

Yet she never told them how BJ had made her so angry that she completely brushed him aside, how her future and her baby's future weighed so heavily on her mind, and how not knowing what to do was driving her insane.

Really, she'd sit there, thinking, *I could raise her. Or BJ could raise her. Or his parents could. Or I could raise her with BJ. Or I could ask my father to help me raise her. Or I could raise her and not let BJ even see her. Or, I could place her for adoption, which might be closed, semi-open, or open.*

Years later, Jess would get a real scream out of the movie *Juno*, where Ellen Page plays a birth mother right around her age. Jess would sit on the couch eating popcorn while watching her life unfolding on the big screen—especially the scenes where Juno walks down the halls at school while everyone is staring at her, and when she's lying in the hospital bed and crying, and her father tells her that someday she will have children of her own. She often watches the movie on Zoe's birthday.

But back then, time passed. Fall turned to winter, and under guidance from Marlys, Jess went from wanting to raise her baby, to not being so sure, to ultimately wanting to place her for adoption. It wasn't a straightforward process because the closer she got to her due date, the more attached to the baby she became, and the more she wanted to keep her. Yet, going through the process of adoption made her feel more at ease and confident in herself and in her decision.

Now she walked down the halls at school not hiding her belly at all and almost flaunting it. As if making a statement, she told everyone, "I chose life"—meaning that she had chosen to give her baby the best life she believed she could while understanding that it was one of the biggest sacrifices she'd ever make.

Fortunately, she had enough credits to graduate early. The last thing she wanted was her water breaking in the middle of class or to have to go back to school after the baby was born. By December, she was even enjoying her pregnancy—both she and her mother were enjoying it together. They just didn't focus on the giving-up part. While Jess's father had urged her, all along, to place the baby for adoption, her mother had told her that whatever she decided, she was behind her 110 percent. When Jess's doubts welled up from within, her mom assured her that she was doing the right thing—for both herself and the baby. She'd tell her that she would probably doubt her decision, until enough time had passed and she knew in her heart that she had chosen wisely.

She also made Jess a "Parenting List" by writing down the pros and cons of both parenting and adoption, and whenever Jess had a tough day, she read it to her, so that Jess would see, in black and white, how many more positives there were for placing her baby for adoption.

PARENTING	ADOPTION
I will be working at McDonald's for 15 years.	Giving a family a child (who couldn't have one).
I will be on welfare for 15 years.	I'll be able to go to college and live happily.
I won't go to college.	She'll be able to get the life she wants and deserves.
No future with a boyfriend.	I will see her again someday.
I won't be able to provide her with everything she wants and needs. I would be with my baby and feel fulfilled, I guess.	I will be able to keep in touch and get pictures and letters, so it's not like she'll be completely out of my life.

Around Christmas, the time came for Jess to select an adoptive family for her daughter. She wanted a married couple, who were Lutheran, and who lived not too close but not too far away. She was interested in having a semi-open adoption, where she would receive annual updates from her child's adoptive parents telling her how her daughter was doing. One afternoon, she met Marlys at Perkins, and Marlys had a stack of portfolios for her to review from prospective adoptive parents.

What a pile of possibilities! Some of the couples had no children; others had four or five. One had snakes, another shared their home with five dogs, and another had a pet iguana. But one couple seemed perfect.

Their names were Sandy and Stephane. Sandy was from Minnesota and was a speech pathologist, and Stephane, who was born in Orleans, France, was an electronics engineer. Jess loved the idea of her daughter being exposed to a different culture, and Sandy and Stephane had already adopted their son, Antoine, who was two-and-a-half, so Jess figured that they knew what she was going through. A meeting was arranged at Perkins Restaurant.

It was raining when Jess and her parents pulled into the Perkins parking lot. When they walked in, Sandy and Stephane were already sitting at a table. Jess immediately recognized them from their photographs: Sandy with her shoulder-length blonde hair and wire-rimmed glasses, and Stephane with his heavy-set build and very short, dark hair. The couple stood up to greet them.

How surreal it was to be meeting people who might eventually become her child's parents. It was sort of like being in a science fiction movie, but Sandy and Stephane seemed warm and genuine, which helped put Jess at ease.

"We understand that you're Lutheran," Jess's mother began.

"Actually, we're Methodist," Stephane said politely with a thick French accent, "but we believe in God and also believe that you make your own destiny. Life is full of surprises, yes?"

Jess and her parents nodded in agreement. Jess liked the sound of Stephane's accent, and she imagined a little girl about three years old sitting on his lap.

"When is your due date, Jess?" Sandy asked and then took a sip of coffee.

"March 26," Jess replied, "I'm 99 percent sure that I want to place her for adoption. I'm having a girl."

"Yes, we were very happy to hear that from Marlys," Stephane said. "How is your pregnancy coming along?"

"Oh, great. I feel very connected to her, and all the tests have come back fine," Jess replied. "It's been unreal being pregnant. I'm sure that I'll never forget it."

Sandy smiled at her, politely. She was a little hesitant, at first, because Jess and her parents had rescheduled the meeting several times, which wasn't such a big deal. However, Jess's parents seemed so uneasy.

"Do you go to church?" her father asked.

"Yes, we do," Sandy quickly responded, adjusting her wire-rimmed glasses, adding, "My sisters and I practically grew up in church. My grandfather was a minister." She thought it was kind of weird for Jess's parents to be grilling them about their morals, values, and Christian upbringing, while Jess was sitting there unmarried and pregnant. She began to wonder if this was going to be a pleasant experience or not.

"Back in France, I was brought up as a good Christian, as well," Stephane added.

"When did you come to the States?" Jess asked him.

"In my late teens, but I didn't come on a boat; I came on a plane," he said.

Jess laughed. She seemed like a sweet girl, they thought. It was just that the whole experience was so weird—being interviewed by a complete stranger to see if they were worthy enough to become her baby's parents. Even though they had gone through a similar experience when adopting Antoine, this situation felt much tenser.

Marlys's presence helped put them at ease. They trusted her.

"I hear that you have a son," Jess mentioned, looking down at her big belly. "I'm having a girl."

"So we hear," Sandy said, grabbing on to good news. "We've always wanted a daughter. One boy. One girl. We'll be good to go."

Stephane could tell, by the way that Jess kept looking at her belly, that she wasn't completely sure that she wanted to place her baby for adoption, which made him a little wary. But he liked her and understood that she had to go through her process, as did they. They all talked for a bit, Jess sharing about graduating high school and her plans for going to college, and that she wanted to become a social worker, and Sandy and Stephane talking about their jobs and their son, Antoine, who was at home with his grandmother.

"I've been thinking about names . . . and like *Emma Grace*," Jess told them.

Sandy and Stephane quickly exchanged glances then wanting to settle the matter now Stephane said, "Well, we already have an Emma in the family. We've been thinking about naming our daughter *Celine*, after my great-grandmother." He continued, "We want a French name that's easy to say and can't be shortened," then added, "Americans always get nicknames. What happens if the child doesn't like it?"

"Grace would be absolutely fine, though," Sandy interjected. "We could name her *Celine Grace*."

Jess thought about it for a minute, and then said okay. She was disappointed but thought that Celine was a pretty name.

Stephane and Sandy were relieved. Then Stephane asked, "What about the birth father, BJ?"

"Oh him . . . he won't be a problem for you," Jess quickly sputtered. "He's not involved in this, at all."

Sandy and Stephane were more than fine with that. They had had a real scare with Antoine's adoption. They were all set to bring him home when his birth father came forward to claim custody of him. He immediately changed his mind, and all was well. However, they learned from the experience that the adoption process could bring some unwanted surprises. As the meeting drew to a close, they felt confident that if Jess went through with her adoption plan, in two months, they would have a new baby daughter.

Jess felt positive too and had made up her mind that Sandy and Stephane were the right parents for her daughter and that she would have a good life with them. She told them that she'd be in touch as soon as the baby was born but didn't invite them to be present for the baby's birth. She knew that for one short day, she would want her baby all to herself.

With an adoptive family in place and her due date less than two months away, Jess was now ready to talk to BJ. She felt compelled to convince him to agree to the adoption. They arranged to meet at McDonald's, but BJ was late, which really ticked her off. When he finally showed up, he seemed as indecisive as ever. Jess pleaded with him to change his mind, going over the benefits of adoption for the umpteenth time, but BJ just said, "I don't know."

When Jess told him that she was in the process of choosing an adoptive family for the baby, it was like salt on a wound. The thought of his child being raised by total strangers was just devastating. Yet at the same time, he also felt that if she was going to be placed for adoption, he *needed to be involved in the process*; as her father, he believed it was his right—his duty—to make sure that she was safe.

Perhaps he should have told Jess that he wanted to be involved, but they left the meeting at more odds than before. Like a time bomb waiting to explode, BJ knew he had to do something but felt that there was nothing he could do but wait. During the following weeks, Jess tried phoning him, but by that point, the tables had turned, and *he* wasn't responding to *her* calls.

Meanwhile Sandy and Stephane began warily preparing for Celine's arrival, painting the guest bedroom pink, putting up curtains, and moving in the crib and rocker, which Sandy had re-covered for the occasion. With two months until Jess's due date, they knew that anything could still happen.

Stephane, especially, wasn't counting his chickens because of what happened with Antoine's birth father and because he hated surprises. An electronics engineer who traveled on business for weeks at a time—and who had scores of engineers reporting to him in the United States and abroad—he swore by having contingency plans, carrying extra credit cards, and using common sense. He lived his life like he played chess: strategizing, making long-term moves, and saving for a rainy day.

To Stephane, everything was a step-by-step process. Yet, he had a heart of gold, and as long as he did what he could in any given situation, he never worried about a thing. He believed that there was always wiggle room in what you do, as long as you played by the rules.

Sandy usually played by Stephane's rules and was very content with having him at the head of the family. A speech pathologist who worked with stroke and traumatic-brain-injury patients, she grew up in rural Minnesota and had spent much of her childhood in church. One of four sisters, she had always dreamed of having a daughter and was absolutely thrilled when Marlys told them that Jess was having a girl.

On March 22, when Jess called them from the hospital, telling them that their daughter had been born, they were ecstatic. Jess was emotional, and it was catching. Even Stephane couldn't contain his excitement. Jess had gone into labor around 1:00 AM and gave birth to Celine the following afternoon at 2:47 PM, with her mother by her side. Celine weighed 5 pounds, 15 ounces and was 19 inches long.

As soon as she started pushing, Jess could tell by her mother's face that she was very excited, which made her push even more. When Celine's little head came popping out, Jess was ecstatic, in bliss. She wasn't thinking about the circumstances; she wasn't thinking at all—she was in the moment, watching the most beautiful little girl being born. Nothing else mattered. Tomorrow, and the day after that, didn't exist.

"I did it. I had a baby," Jess gushed, staring at Celine, her heart bursting with pride. She decided to wait to hold Celine until after the nurses had attended to her and completed their testing, so they left with her, and Jess lay in bed exhausted, her parents by her side.

A little later, when the nurse finally returned and placed Celine in her arms, Jess cried and cried. The nurse mentioned how beautiful and healthy Celine was, and that she

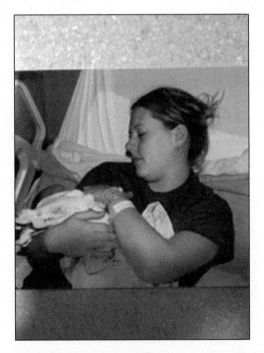

JESS AND ZOE

looked a lot like Jess. Then she explained that Celine hadn't passed her hearing test in one ear, but quickly reassured Jess that this wasn't uncommon in newborns, and that the doctors weren't at all concerned. Jess figured that Celine had failed the test because she was such a small baby.

Shortly after Marlys arrived and gave Jess a big hug, she got straight to the point and explained that for the rest of the day, Jess should expect to be on cloud nine but that the following day, she would probably crash.

Marlys was right.

For the remainder of that day, Jess was in heaven just being with Celine. Jess and her mother tried picking out Celine's features—what she took from her and what she took from BJ. Then she and her mother played cards while they took turns holding and feeding Celine until midnight, when exhausted, Jess slept like a baby herself.

Already on emotional overload, she never called BJ to let him know that she had given birth. She didn't want to deal with the fact that he hadn't agreed to the adoption and open a can of worms on the most incredible day of her life.

Marlys, of course, had let Sandy and Stephane know that Celine had failed her hearing test—and they wondered why—but knowing that happens sometimes with newborns, they weren't concerned. They were more worried about BJ terminating his parental rights in a month from then, if not sooner, and bringing Celine home. This was considered an "at-risk" adoption because BJ had not yet legally surrendered his parental rights. Therefore, if Sandy and Stephane took Celine home and then BJ came forward to claim custody of Celine, they would have to let her go with him. Until BJ surrendered his parental rights, Celine was all set to stay in foster care—the same one at which Antoine had stayed, and Sandy and Stephane had become good friends with his foster parents, Chuck and Lois. Given the circumstances, this situation was ideal.

The following morning, Marlys returned to the hospital bright and early and asked Jess, who was scheduled to check out of the hospital that evening, to pick a time when she would leave, explaining that if she didn't, she might never want to leave. Jess swallowed hard then told her nine o'clock, and Marlys left.

Shortly after, Jess's friends and relatives started filing in. Jess's aunt, one of the first to arrive, snapped a photograph of Celine, and as soon as Jess looked at it, she realized that she only had eleven hours left to be with her daughter.

She knew that she would be allowed to visit Celine in the foster home, but the clock inside her heart had started ticking. Around two o'clock, her "Circle of Trust" stopped by with some Peanut M&Ms and Dr. Pepper, which she really appreciated. But by late afternoon, she was barely holding it together, so her mother asked everyone to leave so that Jess could rest and be alone with Celine. When the clock struck eight, Jess realized she only had an hour left to be with her baby and asked her parents to leave.

The room grew very quiet; except for a few cars honking outside and the rustle of the curtains from an incoming breeze, there were no sounds at all. Jess sat in the rocker catty-corner to her bed. She held Celine, who looked so adorable all wrapped up in her little pink blanket. She wished she could hold her forever.

Gently, she caressed and kissed her tiny face and then sang to her softly, beginning to mourn the life that she believed she would never know.

"I'm so sorry that I have to give you away," she said to her. "I'm so, so sorry." Then she sat there and wept, her grief engulfing her. After the wave of grief subsided and she could speak again, she said to Celine, "I love you and will never forget about you. Please, don't ever forget about me."

Celine stared back at her with her innocent, loving eyes, and Jess, falling, falling, cried out to her mother, who had stepped outside the room, "Mom, read me the Parenting List. Hurry, please." Her mother read the list to her over and over again. Reading it to her forever wouldn't have been long enough.

Ultimately, what got Jess through the night—and many nights to come—was her belief that she had done the best thing for Celine.

Before giving Celine to Marlys, who had arrived right on schedule, Jess kissed Celine on the forehead one last time and told her that she loved her. Marlys didn't say a word; she just squeezed Jess's hand, told her that she'd talk to her soon, and then left with Celine for the foster home. It was exactly what Jess needed. She didn't want anyone to say anything. Then, she and her parents packed up her belongings and left the hospital; Jess was so distraught that her mother practically carried her to the car. In Minnesota, a birth mother must legally surrender her parental rights in order for her baby to be adopted, so the day after Jess left the hospital, she signed the necessary paperwork so that Celine could be adopted by Sandy and Stephane. She braced herself, held her breath, and signed on the dotted line.

Although emotionally spent and feeling like she could sleep for weeks, Jess thought that the worst was over.

* * *

WHEN BJ FOUND out that Jess had given birth—*and hadn't told him*—it was the final blow. Something snapped inside him. He just couldn't believe that Jess didn't have the common decency to let him know that his own daughter had been born. For BJ, it was the ultimate betrayal.

During the following weeks, he felt despair unlike any he had ever felt in his entire life. He started drinking, and the thought of losing Celine was unbearable. The feelings of emptiness, of her being gone and him not knowing where she was, or knowing anything about her life was the hardest part—*he couldn't be there.*

He had breakdowns. One night, he went out with his sister, and the more he drank, the more his emotions came pouring out.

"I have a little girl, and she won't even know who I am," he cried to her.

His sister listened, hating to see him in such agony, yet feeling like she couldn't do anything to help him. She actually thought about adopting Celine herself but wasn't quite ready to have a child.

"For nine months, I swallowed my feelings," he continued. "Shouldn't I have a say in her future, too?" he went on, his anger and resentment continuing to build.

They talked a bit more, and then his sister finally said, "Listen, BJ, you have to do what you have to do."

He knew she was right.

He hired an attorney who explained his legal rights to him and the steps he would have to take if he wanted to sue for custody of Celine. The attorney also began telephoning Jess on BJ's behalf. Jess, now feeling threatened, started responding to his phone calls. Not only that, but Marlys even invited him to the adoption agency to meet Celine.

On April 10, 2004, BJ, along with his parents and his sister, set out for Frost, Minnesota, to see the baby. BJ's dad once again expressed that because BJ wasn't settled in his career, he thought the best thing for BJ to do was sign the paperwork as soon as possible so that Celine could be adopted; however, if suing for custody was what BJ really wanted, he would be there for him.

They entered a cheery-looking room painted pale yellow. An Anne Geddes photograph of babies sitting in flowerpots hung on the wall, and children's toys and books were scattered all around. Below the photograph was a bassinet. Marlys, who was in the room waiting for them, came over to greet them and brought them over to the bassinet. Because Celine was already in foster care, Marlys had picked her up and brought her to the agency to be with them.

"Well, here she is," Marlys said, walking them over to Celine. "She'll need a bottle in about fifteen minutes, if you'd like to feed her. And her diapers are on the shelf."

BJ was transfixed.

"Isn't she darling?" Marlys continued. Then she said that she'd be back in about an hour and left.

BJ looked down at Celine, who was all wrapped up in her pink snuggly, her big, blue angel's eyes twinkling back at him. He wanted to scoop her up in his arms so badly but felt a little nervous, so his mother picked her up and placed her in his arms for him.

His heart melted. *This was his daughter*. He'd felt that way throughout Jess's entire pregnancy, and even more now, he felt an overwhelming need to protect her welling up from within.

Holding her, everything felt good and right. He felt calmer and could think more clearly. He hated the fact that she was in foster care. At one point, the thought did occur to him that she might be better off being placed for adoption, that it would be more stable. Yet, at the same time, because of his upbringing and his experiences with his brother's babies, he just couldn't imagine her being "out there" in the world and not being part of her life. Either way he looked at it, he had a sinking feeling inside.

After an hour, Marlys returned with Sandy and Stephane's portfolio for him to look at. He glossed over it and saw that they were a fine family; but quite frankly, had they been the king and queen of England, he wouldn't have been impressed. When it was time for BJ and his family to leave, he could barely tear himself away from Celine, wishing he could take her home with him and be with her forever.

You have to do what you have to do—his sister's words echoed in his mind. It was then that BJ vowed to be involved in Celine's life from then on in—and not let anybody stop him anymore.

* * *

IN THE WEEKS prior to returning to work, Jess had recuperated at home; visited her mother, who lived about an hour away; and visited Celine at the foster home once a week, which was about an hour away in Blue Earth, Minnesota.

Her first day back at McDonald's, a stranger approached her and handed her an envelope. She knew what it was, immediately: BJ had gone through with his threat to sue her. All of the blood drained from her face, and she started crying. She was right in front of customers but just couldn't help herself. It was such a blow. She wasn't prepared for it. She knew that BJ didn't want Celine to be placed for adoption, but she just didn't think that he would actually sue her for parental custody—that he would actually take things that far. It still hadn't sunk in that he wasn't going to do what she wanted him to. Too upset to remain at work, she asked one of her coworkers to finish up for her, and then went home and told her father what had happened.

"He's ruining my life," she screamed. "We had a plan, and he's ruining it. All of the progress that we've made was a complete waste of time."

Jess's father listened, both of them getting madder by the second.

"What's the point of pursuing adoption or college? I have to be a mother instead. BJ wants to be a good parent. Well, you can still be a good parent, even if you place your child for adoption," she said, beginning to doubt her own decision.

"Don't worry, Jess," her father said. "We'll figure out what the best thing is for you to do."

* * *

IN THE MEANTIME, Sandy and Stephane finally met Celine. They arrived at Chuck and Lois's farmhouse at noon, after having driven for three hours. Lois answered the door, wearing an apron over her dress, with baby Celine cradled in her arms.

They were immediately so taken by Celine's beauty, by the sparkle in her eye, and the way that she laughed and moved; at two weeks old, she was already her own little person. They spent the afternoon entranced by the sweet, alert little girl. The following week they visited again.

Things seemed to be going so well. Lois had taken Celine for a follow-up hearing test, and Marlys told them she passed. They imagined finally letting down their guard. They never wanted to hold back or protect themselves. They wished they could take Celine in their arms and bring her home, but they didn't have the chance. Right after their second visit, Marlys informed them about the trouble with BJ, and then a week after that, he sued for custody.

Stephane was disappointed but not crushed. He knew the drill, and never, even for one second, had allowed himself to think that Celine was theirs. Marlys had already discussed the psychology of birth fathers with him on several occasions. Now, after the suit had been filed, they talked about it on the phone again.

"I know it's upsetting, Stephane, but I'm hoping that BJ will change his mind. Jess kept him away, and now he's asserting his rights, trying to take back some control."

"Yeah, at the eleventh hour," Stephane said.

"His response is fairly typical, but they usually come around," Marlys continued.

Stephane understood the feeling of wanting to be in control. "Well, if BJ wants to raise Celine," he responded, "and has help from his family, I respect that. That is his right."

"Believe me, most birth fathers are not interested in raising their children," Marlys replied.

"Still, so often people *don't* take responsibility for their actions," Stephane continued, "and when they do, I think they should be praised and not judged."

Sandy wasn't quite as understanding and took the whole thing much harder than her husband. It was very difficult not knowing if the baby she already loved was going to be her daughter. But she put the situation in God's hands and tried to think of what had happened as a blessing—that BJ would see that while holding a baby for a few hours was great, being a single father was entirely different. The prospect of feeding her every two hours when she cried at night, and then getting up in the morning and going to work, would be daunting.

After talking with her attorney, Jess went for the jugular, calling BJ on the phone and threatening to never let him see Celine if he lost, which really set him back. Still, even though he knew that he might lose the court case, he had to try. His attorney assured him that if he told the judge how he felt, sharing as passionately about it as he had with her, there was no way that the judge would prevent him from seeing his own child. He was somewhat relieved yet still concerned, knowing that he couldn't negotiate with Jess if the judge took her side.

Jess's attorney also explained that if Jess didn't want BJ to have parental custody of Celine she would have to pick her up from foster care and bring her home—that if she didn't, BJ could claim legal custody over her. Unfortunately, Jess would now have to prove to the courts that she wasn't an unfit mother and that she was capable of taking care of Celine and wasn't abandoning her.

The situation blew her mind. She wasn't prepared; she didn't have a crib or a car seat or baby supplies or anything. However, after talking things over with her parents, it became crystal clear that she would have to bring Celine home to her father's house—temporarily—until she figured out what to do next. Marlys made the necessary arrangements.

Deep down, Jess just knew that she couldn't give BJ parental custody of Celine. If she did, the mother inside of her would have felt like she had abandoned her child.

It would've been like telling the world that she didn't want her own baby, but BJ did.

Choosing an adoption plan for Celine was a completely different matter. Carefully selecting adoptive parents who would love, protect, and nurture her and provide her with a beautiful family and all that goes with it—personally choosing that family for her daughter—*that* she could live with. Sad as the decision had made her, the mother inside of her could go on living, knowing that she had made this painful choice, not out of abandonment, but out of love.

Somehow, things came together. A few of Jess's friends from McDonald's brought over a baby swing and a play-pen. Jess's father contacted human services, helping Jess to apply for welfare, figuring that it would only be temporary. Whenever she felt afraid, he told her, "Jess, this is the right thing to do. No matter what it takes, we have to see this through."

On May 5th, several weeks after she had been served the court papers, with her parents' support and a car seat that she bought at a garage sale securely in place, Jess drove to the foster home to pick up Celine. *Is this the way it's supposed to be?* she wondered as she drove. *Is God telling me to take care of her for good?* She arrived at the foster home barely containing her tears.

Lois, sensing how difficult a situation this was for Jess, gave her Celine's feeding and sleeping schedule, and then Jess left with Celine. Moments later, with Celine sleeping peacefully in her car seat, it hit her. "Oh, my gosh. I have my daughter in my backseat." She drove home, stopping only at the house of a friend whom she trusted for a crash course on caring for her baby. Her friend, who was like a second mother to her own nephew, showed her all the basics, such as how to feed and burp Celine, how to change her diaper, and other assorted tips.

"Always have patience," her friend said, "and remember that Celine won't be sleeping through the night for a long time."

Just a few hours later, she was at home with Celine— whom she'd agonizingly said good bye to just weeks before. It was so hard for her to believe that it was actually happening, that Celine was with her, in her father's house, dependent on her care. Those seven weeks were the most loving, joyful, torturous, fearful, and uncertain weeks of her entire life. She didn't know whether to be Celine's mother or babysitter. She didn't want to become attached to her, but how could she help it? She felt as if her faith was being tested, but never lost hope that BJ would agree to make an adoption plan for Celine.

Once, when Celine was fussing in the middle of the night, Jess traipsed downstairs with her to the kitchen to feed her, figuring that she was hungry. Celine was crying, and Jess, needing her sleep, was terribly grumpy. Well, there Jess was, sitting at the kitchen table in her blue night-gown, feeding Celine, when all of sudden Celine pushed the bottle away, looked up at her and busted out laughing, as if she knew something Jess didn't. She must have laughed for almost a minute. Jess immediately busted out laughing too, told her how much she loved her, and then slept like a baby herself.

As if things weren't challenging enough, Jess soon began noticing that Celine didn't seem to hear things at times. Once, Jess's mother dropped her keys right next to Celine, and she didn't even flinch. Another time during a storm, a crack of thunder shook the house, and again Celine didn't stir. While the nurse at the hospital had told Jess that even though Celine had failed her hearing test the doctors weren't concerned, Jess began worrying. Then, the court day was upon her.

The purpose for going to court was for Jess and BJ's attorneys to officially open up the case. It wasn't time yet for going up on the witness stand or attorney summations. However, unless things changed, that would all be happening soon enough.

Jess and her parents arrived at the courthouse promptly at 9:00 AM, on edge, determined to hold their ground. They met Marlys soon after. She would be acting as the mediator for both sides. The four of them stood and talked for a few minutes, and then Jess, looking out over the balcony to the first floor below, noticed BJ and his parents and their attorney walking into the building.

Jess's heart started pounding. Even though she wasn't advised by her attorney not to talk to BJ, she was afraid of saying very much for fear of saying something she would regret later on. In the five months since she had last seen him at McDonald's, she had built up even more resentment.

BJ and his entourage walked up the stairs and over to where Jess, her parents, and Marlys were standing, and everyone said hello. The two attorneys exchanged a few words and then left, entering a room off the hallway. Wanting to make the best of the situation, Jess's parents and BJ's parents talked cordially for a short while.

At one point, Jess and BJ found themselves sitting together on a bench in the hallway. Jess took in a deep breath then said, "BJ, won't you *please* agree to the adoption? I have to get on with my life, and Celine needs a home."

BJ, also a bundle of nerves and sensing Jess's emotionality, kept his response short. "I'm not ready to do that yet," he replied, by then feeling that things were out of his hands and putting his trust in his attorney.

After taking another deep breath, Jess went on, "We think that Celine has a problem with her hearing."

BJ's eyes opened wide.

"Yeah, she didn't hear my mother's keys when they dropped right next to her or thunder that shook the house."

"Wow," BJ said, not knowing what else to say.

"Most of the time, she's fine, though," Jess continued. "We'll be taking her for a hearing test in a few days. Hopefully, she'll be all right."

BJ nodded in agreement. Yet, throughout the entire conversation, he wondered if he was being too passive and was not fighting hard enough for Celine. Both he and his parents, just like Jess and hers, were beside themselves that day. When Jess had first become pregnant, they were so confused about what might happen and what they could do about the situation. In all their lives, they never could imagine a mother giving up her child. Now here it was happening, and they were a part of it. The whole thing was just inconceivable to them. To make matters worse, BJ's attorney had pulled him aside, informing him that he had a bad judge, one who was particularly big on giving the mother full custody of the child, and that she had seen her do it several times.

When the attorneys returned, after finishing up for the day, everyone reconvened in the hallway. Before leaving the courthouse, BJ's mother went over to Jess, gently touched her arm, and said, "Jess, if there is anything that we can do for you, please let us know."

"Okay," Jess said and turned away, too upset to accept her kindness.

Things went from bad to worse for Jess. Celine's hearing test showed further hearing loss—a much different diagnosis than the one she had been given at the hospital. Jess was beside herself, and after getting home from the audiologist's appointment, she cried for the rest of the day.

She didn't know where to even begin. She didn't know the first thing about hearing loss or what this would mean for Celine. Part of Jess was terrified that Sandy and Stephane wouldn't want Celine anymore—that she would have nowhere to go and would be an *unwanted* baby. The thought was just too much to bear. So, like many of us do at times, she just told herself that the hearing issue wasn't really a big deal, that there could be an easy explanation.

Because Celine hadn't been doing well on her formula, Jess and her parents wondered if she had a milk allergy, which may have caused her ears to be clogged, and that when the allergy was all cleared up, her hearing would be fine. Celine's hearing *did* seem to be fine at times. They switched her formula, and then Jess just crossed her fingers and hoped for the best. She and her parents were both very glad that Sandy was a speech pathologist and would be able to help Celine with whatever she needed later on.

Jess's father, doing his best to keep things on track, invited BJ to his house to visit Celine so that he could try once more to convince him to sign those papers. He purposely invited him to come on the day that Celine had taken her three-month shots, figuring that she would be very cranky, wanting him to see that babies weren't all fun and games—they cry a lot and poop a lot—and hoping that it would get BJ to agree to the adoption.

A week earlier, Marlys had called BJ on Jess's behalf saying that she wanted to talk to him. While BJ had his doubts, his mother thought that it would be a good opportunity to try to straighten things out with her.

However, BJ was right. Marlys walked right into his house and proceeded to tell him that he couldn't possibly earn enough money to provide for Celine because there wasn't enough money to be made in landscaping. She asked him what kind of life Celine would have with just one parent, making it sound like BJ was just another jerk who would fight for his baby out of spite toward the girl he got pregnant. BJ told her point-blank, "I'm *not* that way, and maybe you just found the one situation that isn't like all the rest!" Even BJ's mother thought about asking Marlys to leave.

Contrary to what Jess's parents believed, this was the first time in BJ's entire life when he felt that his parents *weren't* trying to make his decision for him. They had made it very clear to him that this was a decision he would have to make on his own, and they would support him no matter what.

Through the living room window, Jess saw BJ's truck pull up in front of her father's house and then saw BJ get out and walk toward the front door. After he rang the bell, she let him in, hoping for the best. They sat in the living room with Jess's father for about an hour, fussing over Celine and having some tea and cookies.

"Celine's hearing test showed that she has hearing loss," Jess said.

"Wow. I was really hoping that the test wouldn't show that," BJ replied. "Can she get her hearing back?"

"Hopefully. I think that she was born without something she needs that will develop later on and that she'll be fine," Jess explained. "Or she may be allergic to milk."

"She seems to be doing fantastic otherwise," BJ said. He was very sad to hear the news, but in no way did it change his feelings about his daughter.

"Yes, she is," Jess replied.

"She needs a home where two parents can care for her and give her what she needs," Jess's father interjected, firmly, yet calmly.

BJ listened intently.

"We have to think of *her* and put our own feelings aside," he continued. "Won't you please consider placing her for adoption, *please*?"

BJ didn't say yes, but he didn't say no, either.

From the moment that he was with Celine, his thoughts were more fluid, his mind clearer. While he believed that he *had been* thinking of her all along, somehow, the fog finally lifted, and months of agony dissolved into a sad, yet sweet, surrender.

He realized that he had to let her go—that Celine had to move on and find where she truly belonged. He no longer wanted to keep holding her back. Even though he knew that if she grew up with him, she'd have so many wonderful people in her life who would love her, he realized that she needed a father *and* a mother and a family—that having one Christmas celebration would be much better than having two. He pictured her at fourteen and in high school and him asking her what she really wanted as an infant, and her saying, "Hey, Dad, I wanted a family. I wanted to be adopted."

He had to step aside and let it happen.

The thought of her going on without him almost broke him. But he just couldn't take the chance of losing the lawsuit and never, ever seeing her again.

On June 3rd, one week after BJ's visit, Jess figured that her father's plan had worked.

BJ finally surrendered his parental rights to Celine.

Jess's relief was monumental. However, because she had brought Celine home from foster care, she was required to legally sign away her own parental rights—for the second time—which she did, again, feeling once more as though someone had stabbed her in the heart.

When Sandy and Stephane heard that BJ had finally surrendered his parental rights, they were ecstatic. In the backs of their minds, they questioned why. However, it wasn't time for questioning; it was time for celebrating. They were about to leave for France on vacation, which had been planned months in advance. They would have canceled in a heartbeat if Celine had been able to come home with them right away, but because they had to wait another two weeks, in case either Jess or BJ changed their mind—again—they went ahead with their plans.

While in Paris, Sandy and her mother and sister, who had joined them on the trip, went shopping for gifts for Celine at a little French boutique. The place was just darling—filled with all sorts of toys and baby clothes that had French flair. The proprietor, a short woman with dark brown hair and in her late fifties showed them around. Even then, Sandy still had her doubts. She told the woman in her broken French that she was getting ready to adopt a baby and then asked if she could return the gifts if the adoption didn't work out. The woman agreed.

Of all the gifts that she bought Celine, her favorite was a purple and yellow butterfly mobile that had an eighteen-inch wingspan when you pulled the string to make it fly.

Sandy just loved butterflies. They reminded her of her grandfather, who was a minister and also a butterfly expert, and with whom she had been very close. He had loved nature, and one year, during the time of the milkweed and the caterpillars, he made a movie about the life of the Monarch butterfly. At ninety-one, he wrote the script, shot the film, and narrated the entire thing.

Sandy felt his presence when word came from Marlys from overseas that the waiting period was over, that neither Jess nor BJ had returned to contest their decision, and that Celine was finally theirs. That evening they drank champagne, and Sandy wrote in the baby calendar that she had begun keeping for her, "Time elapses for change of mind of birth parents." Her next entry, written on June 23rd, a few days after they had returned home, read, "Placement Day."

They just couldn't believe they were finally bringing Celine home.

Chapter Eight

THE RIGHT THING TO DO

MARLYS ARRANGED FOR Jess, her parents, and three-month-old Celine to meet with Sandy and Stephane at the Caring Pregnancy Center, where Jess's journey with Celine had begun. Jess put on a smiling face, but saying good-bye to Celine at the hospital was a lot easier compared with this. Sandy and Stephane were excited to be picking up Celine, but they felt awkward, too. Based on their adoption agreement, they wouldn't be seeing Jess again until Celine turned eighteen years old or older and then decided that she wanted to see her. Yet everyone was cordial. When Sandy and Stephane asked for an update on Celine's hearing, Jess just told them that Celine had a milk allergy that was clogging her ears, but that it was clearing up and her hearing was fine.

Sandy and Stephane thought that the explanation sounded kind of strange, but neither one of them questioned it. After everything they had been through, all they both wanted was a happy ending, to take their daughter home and love her, and to show her how wonderful life could be. Before adopting Antoine, they'd tried in vitro fertilization for three long years, then made that gut-wrenching leap to adoption, finally realizing that having a *biological* child was not nearly as important as having a *child* and being parents.

Stephane, because of his meticulous nature, would have liked to have asked Jess more questions. He wanted to better understand Celine's condition—to perhaps check first with their pediatrician before bringing her home. But, not wanting to cause Sandy any more distress, and afraid of causing trouble between them, he let things be. At least he knew not to give Celine any milk.

They gave Celine the best of everything. During the first several weeks, things were settling in. Antoine was happy with his new baby sister. Stephane would be away a lot on business—he traveled about 150 days out of the year—but Sandy had taken off from work, for a month, to be with Celine. Still unsure about her hearing, she took her for a hearing test.

The results showed a small hearing loss, which was a bit surprising because when Lois had taken her for a follow-up test, it came back normal. On the doctor's recommendation, they bought Celine hearing aids—the best that money could buy.

Outwardly, Sandy was content, but inside she questioned why things still felt so difficult. She never, ever held back her love—*Celine was her daughter.* Yet, at times, her concern was just overwhelming. Even so, she put it aside and wrote in Celine's baby calendar for the month of June, "We think that you are the most precious daughter we could dream of."

However, several weeks later, she and Stephane got the shocks of their lives. Celine's medical records had arrived in the mail, and in them, a report dating back to when Celine was still living with Jess said: "HEARING LOSS, RECOMMEND HEARING AIDS, SEEK EARLY CHILDHOOD DEVELOPMENT."

Sandy thought, "Oh, my gosh. What's happening with her?" They both were completely beside themselves and just couldn't believe that Jess would have misled them like that. Had they seen that report, they would have asked more questions before bringing Celine home. Even though they appreciated that Jess might have been afraid to tell them what had happened, they wanted the chance to make their own decision. They had suspicions early on about why both Jess and BJ had decided not to parent Celine, but now they were convinced that it was because of her hearing loss.

Although the information was unsettling, it didn't really change anything. They already knew about Celine's hearing loss and were prepared to deal with it. However, the news thrust them on a mission to discover the cause of the loss and to get her the help she needed.

Celine received the best possible care. Working in the hospitals and within the school system, Sandy knew the best doctors and therapists in the area. She took Celine from doctor to doctor and arranged for her to have physical therapy because she also had been diagnosed with having low muscle tone. The situation was far from what she—or any new mother—would wish for, yet, still, she wrote in Celine's baby calendar for the month of August, "total adoration—cutest girl alive."

However, things became even more difficult when Celine's following hearing test showed a significant hearing loss. Sandy and Stephane were crushed because now the picture was changing. Having a hearing loss was one thing, they felt, but if the loss was a symptom of a more serious problem, which the doctor was now suggesting based on the progression of the loss, they had to be sure that they could give Celine what she needed.

There were so many emotions to sort through, and so many thoughts going on inside their heads. They had chosen adoption and were given a baby girl, and it was a beautiful thing, but it was also very painful. They called her their child—she took their name, they were given her birth certificate, and they deeply loved her.

Yet, although no words were spoken, each of them started questioning if they really *were* the right parents for Celine, and if she was the right child for their family.

Still hopeful that with hearing aids they could all get along just fine, they forged on, taking her to a geneticist, who, after finding no signs of a more serious problem, recommended that Celine be evaluated at a renowned hearing center in Omaha, Nebraska. On a whim, she decided to draw some of Celine's blood.

Two days later, they had their answer: Celine had CMV (Cytomegalovirus)—a common virus from the herpes family, such as chicken pox or mononucleosis. Even though only 10 percent of the babies who test positive for it are symptomatic, the symptoms can include deafness, blindness, mental retardation, and auditory processing disorders. The chances of a baby contracting the virus are extremely rare, as the mother has to contract it in her first pregnancy between her twenty-second and twenty-fourth weeks, and even when she does and passes it on to her baby, only 10 percent of those babies ever have any symptoms at all.

Sandy and Stephane were beside themselves and very scared of what it would mean for Celine and for them. They believed that the condition could continue to progress and that Celine might develop additional symptoms, which was what frightened them most. The diagnosis changed everything because now they were not only dealing with the possibility of deafness but also more serious conditions later on.

They were given options and learned that Celine would be a great candidate for a cochlear implant, a sound-stimulation device that can help a deaf child to hear and, as a result, learn to speak. The implant has two parts: one part is inserted surgically into the brain, and the other, a magnetic coil, is attached to the outside of the head and acts like the cochlea, helping to stimulate the damaged nerves that send sound to the brain. A person wearing a cochlear implant can hear sound, but the sound is more robotic than what a hearing person hears.

Stephane and Sandy didn't feel emotionally capable of embracing that.

They knew nothing about being deaf and feared that they wouldn't be able to give Celine what she needed. The language issue would be difficult enough—teaching Celine sign language, while learning it themselves—but with the CMV diagnosis, they kept thinking, *What else?*

Stephane had grown up with a severely handicapped cousin and had seen the pain and hardship that his aunt lived with every day. But he believed that she had been *given* that situation, and had Sandy given birth to Celine, they, too, would have done their best to raise her—no matter what. He felt that part of the magic and mystery of giving birth to a child is parenting *that* particular child.

However, he believed that the *one* benefit of adopting a child was being able to decide whether that child was right for his family. He felt that until three months from now, when he signed the papers in front of a judge legally making him Celine's father, that he had the right—and the obligation—to say no if the situation no longer felt right. He and Sandy had been clear with New Horizons from the very beginning that they did not want to adopt a child with a physical limitation. It was a hard truth to admit, but he believed in always being honest with himself and with others.

Sandy was falling apart, and Stephane was afraid of the situation destroying their family, causing a level of stress that would tear them apart.

One evening, they sat in the living room and talked.

"I don't feel capable of taking care of her but don't feel capable of letting her go," Sandy cried, as if she were deciding which cross to bear.

"It's also all the uncertainty," Stephane added. "And I'm hardly here. It would be all on you."

"What happens if, down the road, she can't even process sign language?" Sandy continued.

"It's not likely, but it's possible," Stephane replied. "It's such a rare condition to begin with."

"And what about Antoine? He needs us, too."

"But she's our daughter," Stephane said.

"Oh, God, please help Celine and help us to know what to do." Sandy prayed.

Stephane reached over and held Sandy for a minute and then said, "Look. Let's see what her next hearing test shows. If her hearing hasn't gotten any worse, then maybe it's a sign that her condition is stabilizing, and that we'll be all right." He paused and then said, "However, if her hearing has worsened, then I think that we have to let her go."

Sandy closed her eyes and nodded in agreement.

Ten excruciating days later, they sat in the examination room next to Celine, who was lying on a table, sedated, an IV stuck in her tiny arm. She was there for a follow-up BAER hearing test to further evaluate the function of her auditory nerve, cochlea, and hearing pathways in her brain. The test was pretty straightforward; the audiologist would increase the level of sound stimulation to her brain, and her responses would be recorded on a screen.

The room was dark and quiet. The woman placed electrodes that would measure her brainwaves on Celine's forehead, scalp, and earlobes, and a small headphone was placed inside each ear.

The audiologist switched on her equipment. A series of clicks, hisses, and other sounds broke the silence. Sandy and Stephane's eyes were glued to the screen. By then, they knew exactly what to look for.

The audiologist began increasing the level of sound stimulation, but Celine didn't respond. Louder and louder, but still no response. Sandy and Stephane sat there, a sickening knowing washing over them, and their hopes diminishing in direct proportion to the sounds that Celine couldn't hear.

In half an hour, it was all over. The audiologist told them that Celine was deaf in one ear, almost deaf in the other, and that, in a month, she'd be deaf in that ear, too.

The word "deaf" reverberated in Sandy's own ears, down to her very soul—"D" for "deaf," and "D" for "dreams destroyed."

Stephane held Sandy close. He, too, had prayed for a miracle. But there were no mistakes—the pieces all finally fit.

"We'll need to do it quickly," Sandy said while they were driving home from the appointment. "It just hurts too much."

"We'll call Marlys tomorrow," Stephane said. "I only hope that she understands." They drove the rest of the way home in silence with Celine resting peacefully in back.

It was September 27th, the day I completed my paperwork for China. The night before, Tim had told me that he wouldn't deny me my daughter.

The following day they called Marlys, who to Stephane's amazement, understood. She asked if they would care for Celine until she was placed in a new home, but Sandy felt that it would just be much too difficult for her to handle emotionally, knowing that any day she'd be saying goodbye to her forever. Marlys arranged for them to bring Celine back to Lois and Chuck's house. Stephane, while believing in his heart that they were doing the right thing both for them and for Celine, was sick with worry about what would happen to her and if she would be okay. He was afraid of her becoming an orphan. However, Marlys assured him that, in all her years of finding homes for children, that had never happened.

Marlys met with Jess to tell her the news. By that time, Jess had been receiving pictures of Celine every week from Sandy and Stephane for four months, so she couldn't imagine what Marlys wanted to talk to her about. She was a wreck and just felt so horrible for Celine, thinking that since Sandy and Stephane had given up their parental rights for her, she was "parentless." (Several weeks after that, when she received their letter explaining that they just didn't have the necessary tools to deal with Celine's deafness, she thought that they were being incredibly selfish.) She asked Marlys if she would have to take care of Celine again, but Marlys just told her to look at what happened as an opportunity to choose a better adoptive family for Celine. She also told her about the CMV, and Jess remembered having a terrible bout with the flu during the twenty-second week of her pregnancy and figured that was when she'd contracted the virus.

* * *

Sandy began gathering Celine's belongings to give to Lois for her foster babies. She believed that, in order to heal, she needed to let go of them as well. It was Sandy's own private Cleansing Stream, the name of a seminar she had taken given by the church that helped her to cleanse herself of negative thoughts and emotions by using prayer, affirmations, and other self-disciplines. She even gave Lois Celine's baby calendar, believing that it just didn't belong to her anymore. She gave away almost everything of Celine's, but she kept the butterfly mobile, knowing that she would need her grandfather's strength to pull her through this crisis.

She had hit rock bottom—giving back her daughter, her dreams being ripped out from under her feet, trusting that there had to be a better family out there for Celine somewhere, but feeling like she'd failed her just the same. She thought of Jess, finally understanding what she must have gone through, too.

It helped that Marlys had embraced their decision, and they took this as a sign that they were doing the right thing;

dropping Celine off at their friends' house—and not into some black hole—was also comforting. When they arrived at Lois and Chuck's house, Sandy hugged Marlys, who had already arrived, and then fell into Lois's arms crying. Even she understood—more than they could know.

* * *

LOIS HELD SANDY while she cried. She had more than just an inkling of what her friend might be going through. It was extremely rare that Lois cared for the same baby twice, yet, when Marlys had called, asking if she could care for Celine, again, she already knew how difficult a situation it was.

She never knew when Marlys would call, but Lois was always available—opening her foster home to any new-born needing a place to stay, giving their birth mother (or birth father) time to decide whether they wanted to parent or place their baby for adoption.

She didn't even mind going without vacations or always staying close to home. She believed it was her destiny, that God had plucked her out of obscurity—the rural town of Blue Earth, Minnesota—and given the opportunity for her to provide a foster home. Usually, foster homes are situated near adoption agencies, but until Marlys's New Horizons had opened its doors just miles from their home in 1987, the closest adoption agency was more than two hours away in the Twin Cities. New Horizons was a Christian adoption agency, no less, which was a dream come true.

It had taken a while for things to all fall into place. Years earlier, Lois had met her son at his foster home, and several months later she and her husband, Chuck, had adopted him. Lois was a nurse, but the minute she set foot in that foster home, she knew that she not only discovered her dream job but also her divine calling. However, her daughter was still young, and New Horizons wouldn't open its office near their home for another thirteen years.

Still, the seed had been planted.

Eight years later, when she had quit nursing and was looking for something else to do, she finally contacted Marlys, and she and Chuck opened their doors. Chuck's first priority was tending their farm—growing corn and soybeans and raising beef cattle—but he adored those babies and always helped Lois with them after coming in from the fields. He also believed that God meant for them to be foster parents and was devoted to doing his part.

Devout Christians and members of the Gideon's, their foster home was their ministry, and caring for the babies was an expression of their love for Jesus. It was a way to serve God and do *His* work. But when a birth mother changed her mind about placing her baby for adoption, they felt the adoptive parent's deep disappointment, as if it were their own.

Their greatest joy, their moment of grace, was when a baby finally went home with its adoptive parents. It meant that their mission with that baby was complete.

That's what fed them. Their true pay wasn't the meager paycheck but was seeing that each baby went to where it truly belonged. It was also a chance to serve God and to form friendships with wonderful people, like Sandy and Stephane, whom they otherwise would never have met.

Pictures of the babies in beautiful gold frames, as well as nativity sets and figurines representing adoption, were placed all over the house. Love was everywhere. The babies, themselves, must surely have known that they were on hallowed ground. Lois took the babies on outings and even to doctor's appointments. She brought her babies everywhere, including church, and always talked about what blessings they were and about the joy they brought to their new adoptive families.

So when Sandy told her, while she was there visiting Celine, that she didn't think that the adoption was going to work out, Lois was heartbroken.

Lois watched it all unfold—Sandy and Stephane's turmoil one day; the hurt in Jess's eyes the next—taking on all of their pain as if it were her own. She had seen some tough situations over the years, but this was a killer. The day that Jess took Celine back was a sad, sad day at their farm. She kept reminding herself that God always had a plan, even when *He* had closed a door but not yet opened a window.

Six weeks later, when Sandy and Stephane finally took Celine home, Lois rejoiced. However, several months after that, when Marlys called, asking if she could care for a five-month-old, Lois knew immediately that the baby was Celine. Sandy had already told her about Celine's CMV diagnosis and the agonizing decision that she and Stephane were about to make.

Lois embraced their decision—she respected their choice—even though thirty years earlier, she and Chuck had made the exact opposite choice. Their son, Mark, whom they adopted back then, had also been diagnosed with CMV and had become deaf.

They'd heard about Mark in December of 1974. The adoption agency had written them a letter about Mark, explaining that he had CMV, and that his development was delayed. But they were still open to the possibility of adopting him, and then they met him. They could easily have said "no" and waited for a different child, but there was something about Mark. It felt so real to Lois—Mark being her son. She looked and looked at his picture while weighing her ability to care for him, along with what she felt in her heart.

She had such feelings for him, yet such concerns. She imagined giving birth to him—knowing that, had that been the case, she would have loved and cared for him no question—hoping that it might help to sway her decision.

It was a difficult three months. But the neurologist had said that Mark's condition was improving, and as they pondered and prayed, nothing made them feel that raising him was beyond their capabilities. They finally decided to adopt him, believing that's what God was leading them to do.

They brought him home in March. It was extremely difficult. He couldn't sit in his high chair without being tied in. He didn't walk until he was two—and Lois had been told that he might never walk at all. She worried about these things and if he would have learning disabilities later on. However, she had no idea that he was losing his hearing. What finally tipped her off was Mark's unresponsiveness when Chuck came into the house, because as soon as Mark *saw* Chuck, he aggressively moved toward him.

Initially, he was diagnosed with auditory agnosia, a condition where a person can hear sounds but can't process them. However, the School for the Deaf, where they had taken him for additional testing, recommended that they treat him as if he were deaf and teach him sign language, which they had to learn as well.

* * *

After Sandy had finally stopped crying, Stephane and Marlys went over Celine's medical information, and Sandy gave Lois all of Celine's belongings, along with her baby calendar. When Sandy and Stephane left, Lois hugged Celine and then made her first entry on September 29 that said, "Celine came to live with foster parents Lois and Chuck."

Then she began signing to Celine.

God, thank you for sending this child to me and not to someone else, she thought, a wave of recognition flooding over her that she had already raised a deaf child and now God had sent her Celine. Her gift to Celine, she realized, was signing to her—and at six months old, that baby desperately needed to be exposed to language!

Over the following seven weeks, Lois's life came full circle, as she relived her experiences with Mark through caring for Celine and applying the same skills she'd learned with him thirty years earlier—something she'd never dreamed she'd be doing. She gained new insight into Mark's condition, which she had craved since he was a child. Mark also had low muscle tone from the CMV, and just as she had helped him to strengthen his muscles and to sit upright, she also helped Celine. She could tell that Celine was losing her hearing and wondered if Mark's process had been similar.

She signed and talked to Celine, even acted things out—knowing that, even if Celine couldn't hear, she should still talk to her. That's total communication. She even gave Celine a "name sign"—a special nickname in the Deaf Culture that people often give to someone. Instead of spelling out a name by hand, a name sign is a blend of the person's name, usually the first letter, and their personality in some way. She learned about it at Mark's school and had given one to all three of her children. Focusing on Celine's aura and beauty, she gave her the name sign of "Pretty Girl."

To the people at church, however, Celine was a lot more than just a pretty girl; she was their social butterfly. At six months old, Celine was so much more vibrant and expressive than the week-old infants they were used to seeing with Lois. Her warm smiles and responsiveness drew them in, making them fall in love with her. They had seen her come and go and then come back again wearing hearing aids. However, knowing that Lois wouldn't talk about it, they never even asked her what had happened.

Sandy, too, wanted to know if Celine was all right and called Lois every now and then to find out. However, knowing Marlys's rules of confidentiality, she never even once put Lois on the spot or made her feel uncomfortable, and Lois respected her for that. She just let Sandy know that Celine was fine and that was it. She didn't even let her know when Celine had found a new family.

PART III

The Roads Converge

Chapter Nine

PROVIDENCE PROVIDES

I DROVE HOME AFTER reading Marlys's email about adopting the deaf baby—thanking God and feeling that at some point in my life, I must have done something good. I was one with the entire universe and with my daughter. I didn't know where she was but felt that I knew who she was—that she was part of me.

But then suddenly I shuddered, remembering that Tim thought we'd be bringing our baby home from China in about nine months from now and might think that it was too soon and wouldn't want to pursue this adoption.

"Dear God," I prayed, "please don't let my daughter slip away from me before she is even mine."

When I arrived home, Tim was in the living room with one of his coworkers, so I paced the house anxiously until the coworker finally left. Tim was sitting on the couch. I sat down on the coffee table, facing him, unable to even communicate. How could I possibly explain to him the profundity of what had just happened?

I took in a deep breath and said, "You're not going to believe this," and handed him my phone so that he could read the email from Marlys.

He read it and didn't say anything; yet, I could tell that his wheels were turning.

"I'll try to get more information," I added cautiously, not wanting to push.

"Well . . . go ahead and look into it," he said.

That was all I needed.

The following day I called New Horizons, and the case-worker with whom I spoke told me that the baby wasn't wanted because she was deaf. How she could just blurt that out was beyond me. But her slip of the tongue turned out to be a blessing because when I told Tim, he became so upset just thinking about what she said that he told me we should go ahead and try to adopt her.

Providence was on my side.

That evening, however, things got really strange. My friend, Ann Marie, not knowing that I had received Marlys's email, forwarded a similar email—the subject line reading, "*Wow, let's go for her!*" Because Ann Marie was also deaf, New Horizons had offered her the opportunity to pursue the adoption as well.

Oh, my God. I was not going to compete with Ann Marie for a baby!

Ann Marie and I had competed for a lot of things over the years and had some good laughs about it, but this was way beyond the realm of comprehension. In her email, she explained that if we both submitted our portfolios, perhaps one of us might become the baby's mother. My cool and logical friend obviously could handle such a thing, but not me. I told her I didn't think I could do it.

However, she was serious; so the following afternoon, the social worker from New Horizons met with us in my office to talk about developing our adoption portfolios for the birth mother to read. (We hadn't developed portfolios for our China adoptions because with international adoptions, you don't need one.) I felt just awful sitting there but had done some soul-searching the night before and was clear about where I stood.

Ann Marie was one of my best friends, and she and her husband, Jon, didn't have any children, whereas Tim and I already had three. In my heart, I felt that I had to step aside and let them try to adopt the baby; I didn't want to be selfish.

"Look, Ann Marie," I said after the social worker left. "I'm going to excuse myself from this process. You and Jon go ahead and try to adopt the baby."

"No!" she replied. "Jon and I decided that if it means you and Tim won't apply, then we'll back out.

At that point, I didn't know what to think. She had really wanted to apply—and now had changed her mind. The whole thing upset me so; I just took off for the women's bathroom and sat down in one of the stalls. I needed to gather my thoughts. Ann Marie followed after me. She peeked over the top of the stall and looked down at me.

I just stared up at her.

"This is *your* little girl," she exclaimed. "Jon doesn't sign. Your home is the perfect home for her." She continued, "Your three boys already sign. She would have the same opportunities that they have had. It would be a much better fit."

I continued listening.

"She'd have unconditional love and parents who had every faith in her ability to grow as a person. She'd be much better off with you."

"Are you sure?" I asked, feeling so guilty about wanting the baby so badly, knowing that she didn't have any children.

"Yes, Brandi. She will be *your* daughter. You and Tim have our full support. Besides, Jon and I have our hearts set on going to China."

Well, all right, I figured, and started laughing as I came out of the stall. After that, Ann Marie and I hugged and then got back to work.

Meanwhile, Tim, after agreeing to pursue the adoption, seemed distant—uninterested even—but I moved forward, ever so cautiously, not wanting to upset the delicate balance I believed that I'd struck with him.

Yet, I'd never wanted anything so much—*never needed anything so much*—and she was right there in front of me, but she wasn't mine yet.

From the moment that I woke up in the morning until I went to bed at night, she was all that I thought about.

I couldn't sleep. I couldn't eat. When all was said and done, I had lost fifteen pounds. There was so much at stake for me.

Trying to remain calm, I filled out the additional paper-work—answering questions such as whether or not Tim and I wanted to have an open adoption and, if so, what kind. They seemed like such important questions, which deserved thoughtful answers, but with no time to spare, I answered them all in fifteen minutes and emailed them back to the adoption agency.

For five incredibly long weeks, I corresponded with Marlys and her staff via email and by phone, trying to get as much information about the baby—whose name they finally told me—her situation and the cytomegalovirus. My first email, dated October 5, 2004, read:

Hi Marlys,

I wanted to let you know that I am working on the portfolio to show the birth mother. I have already gathered my pictures and have started my letter to her. I'm trying hard not to get excited; however, this is so emotional!!

My husband and I are both deaf, and our three boys are hearing. Celine would not only thrive in our home; she would be given the tools required to grow into a successful adult. Her hearing loss is the least of our concerns!

Is her hearing loss the only concern? Did all of her other tests come back as normal? Does she have any other disabilities? Please let me know what the next steps are. Thanks!!!

Holding my breath, Brandi

Next, I began developing our adoption portfolio and went at it with a vengeance, selecting photographs and writing our family story. It seemed as if the very balance of my life was on the line. How on earth would I convince a seventeen-year-old girl from a rural town in Minnesota—who had probably never met a deaf person in her entire life—that her deaf daughter would be better off with us than with a hearing couple?

I was so afraid that our being deaf would work against us—that this young woman would see our deafness as a disability and would want her daughter to be raised by people she considered "normal."

Oh, how I longed to meet Jess in person. One-on-one, I exuded confidence—in myself and in my life. But how do you exude that same confidence on paper? Fortunately, Mark Seeger, a good friend and colleague of mine from Sprint, who had supported me with writing proposals and with whom I'd won several contracts, was in town at the time. We sat around my kitchen island and worked on the portfolio together. At the very least, this was the most important and meaningful proposal I'd ever develop.

Putting myself in Jess's shoes, as best as I could—and without using the word "deaf" even once but using "hearing loss" instead, figuring that it sounded less scary—I explained that Tim and I didn't view our hearing loss as a disability, but rather as part of our cultural identity. That if placed with us, her daughter would thrive because we already lived with hearing loss, and we would provide her with all of the tools that she needed to be successful in life.

I said that she'd have the *right* education and access to communication and all of the available technology—that our home was already equipped with captioning for TV, video technology for the use of the phone, light flashers for when the doorbell rang, and more. Rather than learning about these options for people with hearing loss from parents who, themselves, might be learning about them for the first time, I said that her little girl would have the advantage of immediately being exposed to all of her options—medical and otherwise.

Simple things like sharing a story with her grandmothers, I explained, would be easier because both sets of our parents had traveled that road with us. Her daughter would have generations of support, I said, along with high expectations held for her and a loving understanding of the person she was.

I also shared that we believed in a power that was greater than us, and that each of us has our own unique destiny. Perhaps, I proposed, it was God's plan that she give birth to this baby and that we raise her. I couldn't know this, for sure, I said—that decision was hers alone. But we had prayed for a daughter for a very long time, I explained, and that when I'd heard about her little girl—and the fact that she had a hearing loss—my heart had skipped a beat.

I ended by saying that I hoped to look her in the eye and tell her that if her daughter were placed with us, she would be raised by a family that appreciated her every need. She would learn how to navigate the world around her, on her own, and overcome any barriers that she might

FAMILY PHOTO WE USED FOR ADOPTION PORTFOLIO. IT IS OUR LAST FAMILY
PHOTO BEFORE ZOE CAME TO US.

encounter with confidence. Because, as you must know, I
said, the world can be a difficult place at times.

When I wasn't creating our adoption portfolio, I was
searching the Internet to learn about CMV. Some of what
I read really scared me—kids with feeding tubes, mental
retardation, support groups for mothers—however, knowing that what you read on the Internet isn't always true,
I stayed strong. I reminded myself that it's impossible to
know what the future will bring—that's the risk when having children.

After a couple of weeks had passed without hearing
anything from Marlys, she finally let me know that Jess

had not ruled us out and asked me to be patient, saying that Jess was dealing with a lot of emotions and needed more time to process them.

It was good news. Yet, still craving information, on October 25th, I sent Marlys the following email:

Hi, Marlys,

    I have another question. Why did the first family relinquish Celine? Did all of the medical possibilities from the CMV, in addition to the deafness, overwhelm them?

To which she replied:

    I believe that they were impacted by a number of things. The possibility of total deafness was a great factor, in addition to possible developmental learning delays. As you know, different people are impacted by different "handicaps." What for some of us may be a hill, to others may be a mountain. I may have difficulty parenting a child with major physical needs, but better able to handle a child with emotional needs.

I wrote:

    I am under the impression that Celine's eyes and liver have been tested, and that she has had a brain scan and everything turned out to be normal. I also understand that she has a 25 percent chance of eventually losing her vision. That seemed small to me, and I wondered if after she had her vision tested that the concern was even less?

To which Marlys replied:

> *By routine, the exam for liver, eyes, and a brain scan are done. In a small percentage of cases, all of these areas can be impacted. That being said, there are only a minute percentage of infants that are positive with CMV! All of Celine's testing shows no impact, and the actual test results would be shared with you, if the biological mother selects you as the adoptive family.*

I wrote:

> *Celine is probably seven months old by now, and I would like to ask how she is doing. Is she developing normally in size? It is so critical that she be exposed to language as soon as possible! Can I call you? I want to understand the chain of events that happened in this baby's life. . . .*
> *Brandi*

I thought about my little girl just lying there and no one communicating with her; so many concerns I couldn't possibly have expressed were running through my mind. Did they realize that a deaf infant could be severely slowed down in acquiring language unless *early* and effective measures are taken—unless she is given *sign language*? Did they understand that she must be exposed to fluent signers? That she needs parents who will communicate with her *properly*, who know how to address her, and who use dialogue and language that advance her mind?

I may have been getting ahead of myself, after all she was still a baby, but did they understand that as she grew, she must be asked probing questions, be introduced to logic, cause and effect, and to a conceptual world that would give meaning to her life, just like hearing children are? That she must learn to understand symbols, the past and future, relationships, and hypothetical events? How to deal with things at a distance, arrive at new versions of reality, and verbally rearrange situations, which, in themselves, resist rearrangements?

Who would introduce her to imaginative literature and help her to juxtapose objects and events far separated in time and space, so that she could turn the universe symbolically upside down?

All of us have an innate ability for language. But this ability is only activated by someone else who has already had language training. When I traveled around the country as Miss Deaf America, I learned that most hearing parents with a deaf child feel powerless when confronting such a communication barrier. I was so fortunate that my parents had learned how to sign. So many deaf kids grow up as strangers in their own homes.

Tim has often talked about being in the fourth grade and having dinner at his friend William's house, and his parents, who were hearing, just sitting around the table and talking while ignoring William and Tim the entire time. To this day he has never forgotten it.

As Miss Deaf America, I saw through my travels that poor linguistic ability is common in prelinguistically deaf children, like Zoe. They can have a limited vocabulary, lack concreteness of thought, and have difficulty with reading and writing later on.

Their cerebral development can even be altered; maturation of their brain can be delayed. When they become older, they can have difficulty with formulating hypotheses, refer to objects in the immediate environment only, and be confined to a preconceptual, perceptual world. It may be hard to believe, but some deaf children have difficulty understanding the concept of "question." They know the answer but just don't understand what a question is.

And what about the connection between language and thought? People rarely think about that, hearing people especially, because they automatically have language just by hearing. But *language* is what makes thought possible. People speak not only to tell others what they think but also to tell *themselves* what *they* think. Speech is a part of thought.

Well, just as hearing people need the language of speech to be able to think, deaf people need the language of sign. Sign *is* our language; without it we won't be able to think. Just as a hearing child must learn to speak at a normal, early age for his or her intellect to develop properly, so must a deaf child learn to sign. For it is language, rather than *what kind of language,* that nurtures not only linguistic competence but also intellectual competence.

Only when my little girl learned how to sign would all else follow: a free flow of information and conversations, reading and writing, emotional growth, and then speech.

However, if she didn't learn how to sign, everything else would be in jeopardy.

I emailed Marlys, again, regarding my concerns. Her response, which was curt—but which I appreciated, as she had to remain neutral—was that while Jess was thinking things over, she would do her best to educate Jess about the needs of her baby.

To complicate matters even further, the adoption agency stipulated that if we adopted Celine, we would be required to provide her with a cochlear implant because it was determined that she was a good candidate for one.

Well, Tim was really angry. Number one: he resented the adoption agency dictating to us how to raise our own child. Number two: he and a good part of the Deaf community are against cochlear implants because they don't believe that being deaf is a disability or that they need to be fixed. He says it would be like white people trying to paint African American people white. Some deaf people also view the use of cochlear implants as a loss of their Deaf Culture.

The reason for this is that when a child is given a cochlear implant, the child's parents (who are usually hearing) are told by the mostly hearing professionals to only talk to their child and not sign to them. Research has shown that deaf children who sign often have speech delays, something their hearing parents don't want for them (although other research has shown the opposite). I completely understand; in a similar way, my own mother wanted me to continue speaking after I became deaf. Unfortunately, this kind of thinking can perpetuate the notion of deafness as a defect, with hearing being the ultimate goal.

Tim wanted his daughter to feel good about herself, exactly as she was—and not feel "less than," or that she had to hear to be somebody. He also believed that the time that she spent learning how to speak in school would be better used by learning math, reading, history, and science, along with our language of ASL.

I completely embraced where Tim was coming from. However, the whole issue brought me right back to the AG Bell Conference years before when Eric's father had said that he wanted Eric to speak *and* sign, that he wanted him to have both—he wanted him to have a choice. After all those years, I finally grasped why his words had meant so much to me.

I, too, wanted my daughter to have both—audiological training and sign language. I wanted to encourage her speech, so that *she* could have a choice, so that she could have total communication. I knew that being deaf would always be an integral part of who she was, but I didn't want it to limit her.

But my daughter's speech wasn't my concern. October just dragged on. Like an automaton, I went to work every day, forced smiles, took care of the kids, put one foot in front of the other, and kept things copasetic between me and Tim. I was afraid to feel and afraid that if the adoption didn't work out I would never get over it. Every day, I prayed to find solace and inner peace.

Yet, I'd never felt closer to God. I believed that God was with me, listening to me, and hearing my request. I talked to God *all day long* about my little girl. And I prayed that Jess would pick me as her daughter's adoptive mother.

At the time, our family was attending a deaf church with a very small congregation, and many of my colleagues from Communication Service for the Deaf were parishioners there as well. I also asked them to pray that Jess would pick me. I stood up in front of the entire congregation and just asked.

"May this baby find the proper parents in Brandi and Tim," we all prayed.

At work, I met with people in my office, and I asked other people to consider me in their prayer groups. Whenever Marlys emailed me with an update, I immediately forwarded it to my prayer chain—a small group of church elders, with whom I was in regular contact—and they prayed for me.

By the first week of November, my patience was wearing thin, so I called Marlys and asked if she had any news. She had just been getting ready to call me.

Jess wanted to meet me.

At that moment, I knew that little girl was mine. I just wept and wept. Developing my portfolio had been a mountain; meeting Jess would be a hill. I ran straight upstairs to Tim's office and shut the door.

"This is it," I said through my sobs. "We have a daughter."

I felt such an intense identification with that baby, such an immediate, intuitive bond. While I imagined that Jess loved Celine very much, I believed that because Jess was hearing, had she tried to see her daughter's future, she'd have seen a black veil of limitations.

But when I saw her future, I saw her challenges, her accomplishments, and her wonderful life. I didn't know the particulars, but before I'd even laid eyes on her, I understood her.

I knew that it was in God's hands; I had done all I could. A deep sense of calmness and relief just washed over me, one I had never known before—peppered only with sheer excitement and the need for even more information.

When? Where? How? Who would be there?

Two days later, on Friday evening, November 5th, Tim and I, along with an interpreter, drove to Fairmont, Minnesota, to meet Jess and her parents at Perkins Restaurant. Jess and her mother had already arrived and were sitting at a booth when we entered the restaurant. Tim and I didn't know what Jess looked like, but she and her mother recognized us from our adoption portfolio. I remember thinking how pretty Jess was. In a way, we could have passed for sisters, with our light-colored hair worn swept to the side and our similar coloring, although her face was rounder than mine and my eyes are blue. Hers are hazel, and when she smiled, she lit up the room. How I came to cherish that smile.

We went over to their booth and sat down. Jess's mother starting crying, which made me cry a little, too.

There would be seven of us in total, with Marlys and Jess's father, who arrived shortly, so a small table was attached to the booth.

And so the meeting began. It was a bit awkward for Tim and me at first because Jess's parents hadn't seen Marlys since Sandy and Stephane had relinquished Celine and she had gone back to foster care, where she was at the time, and they were very angry with them. They wanted to know why they had let her go and how they could have done such a thing. Tim and I just listened uncomfortably while Marlys tried explaining that what had happened was all for the best.

As the evening progressed, Jess told us about her life and then said, with sort of a triumphant look in her eye, that BJ wouldn't be a problem for us. She also assured me that she would go through with the adoption, saying that otherwise, she would have to quit college, go pick up Celine from foster care again, and raise her on her own, which she was clear she did not want to do.

Tim was much quieter than usual. Even though we had an interpreter with us, he figured that it was best to leave the communicating to me—especially when the topic of a cochlear implant came up; he didn't want to jeopardize our chances of Jess choosing us as the adoptive parents of her baby, thinking that it might be a deal-breaker.

However, I told everyone that if Celine was a good candidate for a cochlear implant, I wanted her to have one, that I was open to exploring all options. The conversation then turned to Celine's cerebral development. The topic seemed to make Jess and her parents worried. I just looked Jess straight in the eye and said, "There's nothing wrong with Celine's brain. She's absolutely fine."

As the meeting drew to a close, Marlys told Jess that she didn't think she should make a decision immediately, but that she should go home and think about everything that we'd talked about and then decide if she felt that Tim and I were the right parents for Celine. On the way out, I asked Marlys to please let us know as soon as Jess had decided.

Chapter Ten

WAITING ALL OUR LIVES

I T DIDN'T TAKE long for Jess to decide. The following evening I received an email from Marlys, saying that she had chosen us to be Celine's parents.

I was ecstatic! Finally, after years of waiting, only a few hours and a tank of gas kept me from my daughter. I just couldn't wait to meet her; I had no idea what she even looked like.

It turned out that Jess had loved our portfolio, and after meeting us, just knew in her heart that we were the right parents for Celine. At first, she was a little afraid to trust herself because she had been sure that Sandy and Stephane were "the ones." But finding her courage—as she'd done so many times before—she picked us without any input from her parents, feeling that this time, she just had to decide for herself.

Marlys had emailed me Lois and Chuck's phone number, so I called and we arranged for Tim and me to drive up to Blue Earth, Minnesota, the following Tuesday to meet Celine. I could barely contain myself until then.

Bright and early Tuesday morning, after dropping the boys off at day care, we were on our way. I thought of that ride as my "going into labor" because when we arrived, my daughter would be born to me. After two-and-a-half hours—which felt like an eternity—we pulled into the driveway of a quaint, white farmhouse that must have had close to a dozen cats roaming around outside.

It's uncanny. I've always thought that foster homes should be on farms—perhaps because farms have such a wholesome appearance. They're so all-American, with the flowers and the white picket fence—the kind of home that you'd want to grow up in, where it's safe and warm and the love is real.

Lois and Chuck's foster home seemed exactly like that.

When I got out of the car, I saw Lois inside the house, standing right by the open front door and holding Celine. I felt a sudden, urgent need to run up and take the baby in my arms and kiss her. I got out of the car and sped up the front steps into the house, holding out my arms, and Lois said to me, "Would you like to wash your hands before you hold her?"

I quickly went into the kitchen and washed them and then she gave me Celine.

My God, she was so unbelievably beautiful—blonde hair like Blake's and mine and blue eyes like all my boys, as if she were our biological daughter. And she looked so happy.

I was in such a daze and so focused on Celine that I didn't even realize that Lois had started signing to me. While we were there, I voiced and signed, and Lois signed back. She hadn't mastered ASL and couldn't understand Tim, so I interpreted for her. Although her signing was limited, we all managed just fine.

I liked Lois from the minute I met her. She was very warm and good-natured and so easy to talk with. She was like a cuddly grandma and *the* ultimate caretaker—someone who feeds you milk and chocolate chip cookies, yet is extremely professional.

She invited us into the living room, and for the next two hours, we chatted and played with Celine. Tim and I were right down on the floor with her—in heaven. He was with her the entire time, but I also spent time talking with Lois. My mission that day, in addition to meeting my daughter, was finding out as much information about her from Lois as I possibly could—not just medical and physical, but also personal.

I just dove right in, asking her point blank, "What happened to Celine? What was Jess's story? BJ's? Sandy and Stephane's?" I just had to understand my daughter's past, knowing that one day she would ask me about it.

Lois would give me bits and pieces of information and then just clam up. She said that it had been very hard on Sandy and Stephane—and I could feel her deep compassion for them—and then, in midsentence, she just stopped.

She clearly was walking a very fine line between what she would and wouldn't share. She didn't want to betray their confidence. Yet, she also respected my need to know.

Meanwhile, Tim was holding his little girl like his life depended on it.

All those weeks, I had thought that he was removed from the adoption process and only began to get involved the day we met Jess. I didn't think it had registered with him that there was a baby out there, one who might actually be *our daughter*—that all along he was thinking, "Yeah, Brandi, whatever. I already have three kids, and now I'm going to have four."

I thought he was oblivious to how much time and energy I'd spent developing our adoption portfolio and communicating back and forth with Marlys. I thought that, even though he knew that the baby was deaf and had agreed to move forward, he was doing it for me.

I was wrong.

Tim had wanted to adopt Celine, but knowing that we were just one of several applicants, he didn't want to get his hopes up. He couldn't see how Jess could turn us down, but you never know. He also knew how deeply disappointed I would be if things didn't work out, so he just dealt with it all by being removed.

Yet, the moment he laid eyes on Celine he thought, *My little girl—in so many different homes. She doesn't deserve that.*

He felt nothing personal against Lois and later saw how deeply she had loved Celine; it was just the principle of the thing. He didn't want his little girl in a foster home—he wanted her home with us.

He was lying on the floor next to her—he looking at her and she looking at him so innocently and helplessly. He was thinking that all she ever wanted was a good home, a good family, and parents who could give her what she needed, when all of a sudden, she just reached up and grabbed his finger.

His heart melted. At that moment, she became his daughter, too.

It was as if she were saying to him, "You're my dad," and she was his little girl. Instantly, the overwhelming issue of having too many children disintegrated into thin air; all his worries and anxiety were gone, replaced by a full and vibrant picture of us as a larger family.

When it was time to leave, all I wanted was to pick my daughter up and bring her home. However, the child protective laws required that we visit her in foster care two more times before the paperwork could be completed and we could bring her home. It was the longest two weeks of our lives.

Knowing how much I still thirsted for information, Lois suggested that, before beginning our long drive home, we stop by New Horizons' main office, only ten minutes away, to pick up Celine's medical file, which we did.

Well, I suppose that everyone is tested, at times, and this was one of mine.

The file was three inches thick!

I'd never seen so much medical information in one pile, with terms like "hypotonia" and "mucosal thickening." It really scared me. The whole way home I just sat there flipping through pages of information I didn't understand. One CAT scan of the baby's brain said that she was losing her hearing and another said that there was a white mass—*scarring on her brain*—which scared me the most.

I became concerned about the kind of care she would require and if I was taking on more than I could handle. Looking back, I can really appreciate what Sandy and Stephane must have gone through. I just stared and stared at her pictures, which were also in the file. By the time we pulled into our driveway, I had worked myself up into a frenzy.

To calm my nerves, I called my sister-in-law on the videophone and showed her the pictures. After that, I went to the kitchen and told Tim my concerns.

"She's our daughter," he said. "She's going to be fine."

That was it. End of discussion.

From the moment she grabbed his finger, he was tied to her. There was no way he'd ever let her fly away or leave her stranded. But for just a split second, the thought flitted through his mind, and he imagined if he did abandon her and met her in twenty or thirty years—perhaps her life was great, and perhaps it wasn't.

But he sure wasn't going to take that chance.

I remember feeling so grateful that he felt that way, and years later I marveled at how we had really held each other up; when one of us had doubts, the other remained strong.

Wanting to better understand what was in the file, I had emailed my good friend Sheila as soon as we arrived home. Sheila was a nurse and the director of a large regional health care facility in Watertown, South Dakota. I asked her if she'd look through the file and give me her opinion. Sheila and her husband lived about an hour and a half north of us, near the lake house that Tim and I owned with Ann Marie and Jon.

The following day, she left work in the middle of the afternoon and drove down to our house. I'd left the door open for her.

"Oh, Sheila," I said, handing her the file as she came in.

She gave me a big hug and said that she would read over the file to give me her initial thoughts, and then take it home to read it more thoroughly and also give it to one of the doctors at work to read.

"What does all of this mean? Is she going to be okay?" I asked, needing to prepare myself in case my little girl was going to be mentally challenged or disabled in any way.

Sheila just said to me, "What is disabled, Brandi? Aren't we all disabled in some way?"

Then we stood around my kitchen island reading the file together, me asking questions, and Sheila, ever so calmly, answering them ever so simply.

Sheila explained that "hypotonia" meant low muscle mass and that Celine's hypotonia was not attached to a brain injury but "failure to thrive," meaning that with physical therapy, she'd probably be just fine. She also said that Celine definitely had had "an incident"—that she had been affected by a virus or some other malady—but that it didn't look like it was ongoing.

"What about the scarring on her brain?" I then asked, terrified.

"Let me put it this way, Brandi," she said. "Didn't you have meningitis?"

"Yes," I replied.

"Then I bet that you have the same thing on *your* brain. It's from the virus. It's what happens when you get a fever like that," she explained.

"*My God, she's just like me,*" I said, all my worries flying right out the window.

I knew then that Celine was going to be all right. It was as if Sheila had said to me, "She's your daughter, Brandi. She belongs with you."

Just then, what my mother had said to the doctors, when I was so sick as a child, came flooding into my head, "She will not die, doctor. She will not die."

My mother's knowing had become mine; her strength became my strength.

I didn't care what the doctors said or what I read in the medical records. The voice that was claiming that she would be all right was much louder than the voice that had concerns.

Just as with all my children, my expectations for her were high, and I knew that whatever the future brought, I would rise to the occasion and deal with it. I understood this was a giant leap of faith, but I wasn't looking back. The pull toward my daughter was just much too great for me to do otherwise.

Sheila went on to say that nothing ominous had been written in the report at all. She explained that at seven months old, Celine was what she was, and even though she would eventually become completely deaf, the report didn't conclude that there would be any further complications.

After Sheila and I finished our discussion, we had a glass of wine and then hugged, talked, laughed, and cried.

It's strange, but at the time, it didn't even seem like I had made a choice. Yet, I had just made one of the biggest choices of my entire life. I understood that there was a chance that my daughter might have a learning disability, but any child could. My boys could have had learning disabilities. You just teach the child differently.

The following day, I splurged on a shopping spree for girls' clothing. No more looking the other way! I just shopped till I dropped—I bought a pink velvet dress and red velvet jacket from Baby Gap and brown spotted pants with a burgundy hoodie from Gymboree. And lots more. It was absolutely a dream come true. I must have charged more than five hundred dollars on my credit card that day.

Clothes and fashion have always been my indulgence. My grandmother was a seamstress in New York City back in the 1940s, during a time when women weren't in the work world the way that they are today. I inherited my fashion sense from her—through her genes and by her example.

She was a very classy woman—always done up beautifully and looking great. And she was so strong. I think

that I'm in touch with my female strength and feminin-
ity because of her, too. She instilled that yearning in me
for a daughter, someone to pass along my sense of what
it means to be a powerful deaf woman and everything I
had ever learned. I was about to have a daughter to buy
clothes for, go shopping with, and do all that girly stuff
with. Four years later, when my daughter was in preschool, she would win the award for being "most fash-
ionable," and the first word she finger spelled would be
"mall." That's my girl.

She was wearing her brown pants and burgundy
hoodie outfit the day we brought her home. It was Friday,
November 19th, when we picked her up at the adoption
agency.

ZOE ON PLACEMENT DAY WITH FOSTER PARENTS LOIS AND CHUCK

Tim and I went alone, just as we had always gone alone to the hospital when each of the boys was born. We felt it was "our" time with the new baby.

When we arrived at New Horizons, Jess and her parents were already there visiting with Celine. We said hello briefly and then went into Marlys's office to sign the adoption papers—where we agreed to send updates about Celine to Jess and BJ, through New Horizons, every year on her birthday.

After we were finished, Tim and I joined Jess, her parents, and Celine in the other room. I think it had finally sunk in for Jess's parents that Tim and I were deaf because Jess's father asked us how we would know when Celine cried. We hadn't brought an interpreter with us, so communication wasn't the best. However, I reminded them that we had already taken care of three babies and that we had a baby-cry signaler that would flash whenever she cries. We had previously told them that our entire house was equipped with everything we needed—lights for the phone when it rang, a videophone, and captioning for the TV. I now added that some deaf people even have a flashing light for the doorbell and fire alarm but with three hearing kids and a dog, we didn't need them.

Then I gave Jess the letter I'd written her, which said the following:

Jess,

I have nothing but admiration for you. What you have been through these past several months makes me shudder.

What a great amount of courage and strength you've shown to find the best home for your daughter. I know how angry and disappointed you must be with Sandy and Stephane, but their choice not to adopt Celine has led her to us.

I promise you that Celine will have the best of everything. I thank you for trusting us with her—for giving me the chance to be her mother. You will always be the mother who gave her life, and when she is old enough I will tell her that she is blessed to have such an amazing birth mother as you! You will always be a part of her, and she a part of you.

The best thing that you can do for her now is to go after your dreams. Finish your education—there is so much power in that. Be true to yourself. I will teach her to do the same. If you have the opportunity, take sign language classes. If you decide to pursue your masters in social work, check out Gallaudet University.

I want nothing but the very best for you, Jess. You are a beautiful girl with a million-dollar smile that lights up the room—that's priceless. Use everything you've got to make your mark on the world. Celine and I will be rooting for you.

Brandi

Jess didn't read the letter but put it in her purse. Then we all talked a bit more, and finally she gave me a look that said, "It's time," and stood up and placed Celine in my arms. I immediately started crying.

"Don't cry," Jess said.

But I just couldn't stop.

Through my tears, I saw her and her parents walk out the door.

I immediately turned to Marlys, asking her how Jess could leave without even shedding a tear, and she replied, "It's her third time doing this, Brandi. Each time she has gotten stronger."

As I wiped away my tears, I started thinking about the gifts I'd given to Tim and the boys over the years—for birthdays, Christmas, or no reason at all—and the thought I'd put into making them meaningful. Here was a young woman, I realized, who didn't even know me and who had had such painful experiences, yet she found it within herself to choose me—to place her daughter in my care—which was one of the greatest gifts of my entire life. To this day, I well up just thinking about it.

That's when I vowed to legally keep our daughter's name, *Celine Grace*.

Originally, I had wanted to change her name to *Destiny Zoe*—Destiny, for obvious reasons, and I liked the ring of Destiny Zoe. However, Jess didn't want us to change her name, and in Minnesota, the birth mother has that right. I had figured that in six months, when the adoption became finalized, I might legally change it then.

But watching Jess leave, I realized that honoring her wishes was a lot more important than changing our daughter's name. Jess allowed us to legally add the name Zoe, which we did, making her name Celine Zoe Grace.

But we just call her Zoe.

After we left New Horizons, I placed Zoe in her new tan car seat and sat next to her for the three-hour ride home. When we arrived, my friend Kelly was waiting for us with the three boys—video camera in hand—and taped us as we came through the front door. It was around 8:00 PM. The boys were so excited; Blake and Chase had already met Zoe at Lois and Chuck's farm, but Austin hadn't come along. The moment he saw her he reached out for her and just kept saying, "She's my Zoe."

By the time I finally put Zoe to bed that first night, it was already ten o'clock. She slept in the same room each of the boys had slept in as infants, only with pink crib sheets instead blue or green. At 2:00 AM she awoke, so I went into her bedroom and took her out of her crib, and we sat

She's my Zoe. Austin and Zoe.

<small>BLAKE AND CHASE HOLDING ZOE WHEN SHE ARRIVED HOME</small>

on the floor playing and doing her physical therapy exercises. Better get to work, I figured. Then, I gently put her to sleep and went back to bed. After that, she always slept straight through the night.

The following morning, Tim and I were sitting at the kitchen table, and I was holding Zoe. We were just chatting, and at one point he said, "I feel like you just gave birth to her," and I thought, *I told you so!*

I remembered his comment a few weeks later when taking Zoe to the audiologist for a follow-up appointment. At one point, the woman just looked at me and said, "Not many people would want to adopt a child like her."

I was in complete shock. I just couldn't understand how she could say such a thing—*or think it*. I'd wanted

Zoe *so badly*; no one wanted her more than me. I thought that what she said was rude, insensitive, and inappropriate, and I must have been feeling pretty spent from all the changes, because if anyone ever said that to me today, I would let them have it.

But later that day, I realized that there was truth to what she had said because suddenly her comment became yet another confirmation that everything was meant to be. She had only reinforced for me that Zoe and I belonged together. I think that I was then able to see what she had said not as a judgment but as a statement of fact.

Judging is so easy. After Sandy and Stephane had let the baby go, some of their friends had felt that what they had done was very wrong. Still others wondered what

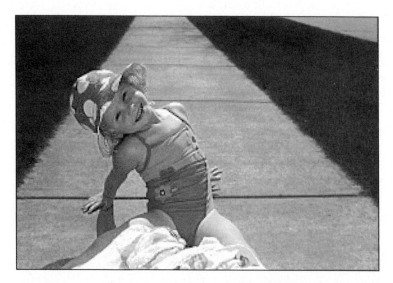

ONE OF MY FAVORITE PICTURES OF ZOE

had taken them so long. I think they all missed the point, because in the divine order of things, there are no rights or wrongs. Judgments aren't necessary. What was wrong for them was perfect for Tim and me. Their acting on their truths allowed for the unfolding of true harmony.

It didn't stop unfolding. The following March, after Zoe had been with us for four months and was just about a year old, Sandy wrote us a letter in response to a letter that I had written to them several months prior, thanking them for taking such good care of Zoe. They had given Tim and me permission to contact them via the adoption agency, and I so wanted them to know how grateful we were for all they had done for her. Her letter said the following:

Brandi,

I have wanted to write to you since we received your letter, but didn't get it done, obviously. I want you to know that we are so pleased that you were able to adopt Zoe. We loved her with all our heart, but knew that in her best interest, we just couldn't keep her. We knew nothing of the Deaf World, and knew that that was where she was headed. We truly couldn't be more pleased with what Lois and Chuck have told us about your family.

I can tell you that it was the hardest decision we've ever made, and the worst day of my life was the day when we took her back to Marlys. But we saw God start to work immediately after our decision was made.

I have to say that it was a little shocking to find out that she's here in Sioux Falls. But then that is where the best family for her is. After getting over the initial shock, I realized that your family could do more for her than we could. We have all the love in the world for her, but not the ability to sign or knowing much about being deaf. You can give her everything in that domain.

We have no regrets with our decision. We know it was of God. Sometimes I wonder why we had to go through all the pain, but there was a reason.

Someday, I hope that you will let us see her again. We would never want to impose on your life with her, but I really love her, and miss her. Antoine and I still talk about her occasionally. He will say, "This is a toy that Celine would have loved." He knows that her name is now Zoe, and asks where she is. I think he thinks about her but is over the missing part.

I am not yet ready to see her. I know that our decision was right, but my heart still hurts a little. It is easier, knowing that she has a family like yours. Thank you for who you are, and for loving our Celine Grace, and now your Zoe.

Sandy, Stephane, and Antoine, too

The following May, Sandy was ready to see Zoe and came to visit us with Stephane, Chuck, and Lois. Tim and the boys were at the lake house that day, so it was just me and Zoe. When I found out that they lived just a couple miles from us, I was absolutely amazed. For so long, I had thought that we'd be traveling to the other side of the world to find our daughter; yet, there she was, right in our own backyard.

I was so curious to meet them, as they me. Lois, God bless her, was our stand-in interpreter. Although Stephane had been at peace from the moment he had found out about our family and that we were deaf, I think that Sandy needed to actually see how well Zoe was doing—how she was running around, playing, and signing to me, to really be at peace. The most telling moment was when I took her upstairs to Zoe's room and she saw the beautiful butterfly on the wall, just above Zoe's crib. It was one of those 3-D ones, made out of yellow and purple fabric, with a touch of pink—just like the butterfly mobile she'd once purchased to hang above Zoe's crib. Talk about a confirmation. Sandy took it as a sign that they really had made the right decision—that Zoe had flown to where she truly belonged.

It's ironic, but it wasn't until years later, when I began writing this book, that I discovered that butterflies are deaf.

"This thing called inspiration [is] rather like a butterfly . . . deaf and blind, but luminous."

—CAMILO JOSE CELA, 1989 NOBEL LAUREATE

EPILOGUE

I NITIALLY, this book was supposed to be about Jess, BJ, and Sandy and Stephane, who had all so lovingly cared for Zoe before she came to Tim and me, and the struggles they went through in making their agonizing decisions to let her go. Although I didn't yet know the details of their stories, part of me knew that each of them had made their difficult choice out of love for Zoe—for whom they believed she was then and would eventually become—and that it was what she deserved.

Delving into their stories, I came to see how each of them had made their choice out of their desire to follow their own truths, and that by doing so, what they did also had to be right for Zoe. I believed all of that in my very soul. When I understood how innocently Zoe had rippled through each of their lives, shaping and defining their lives and each of them as individuals to better know who they really were, I was in awe of them, of her, of myself, and of the awesome mystery that brought Zoe and me together. I could better see how she has rippled through my own life and still does, changing me, inspiring me to grow, always making me a better person, as children often do.

As I honored their decision-making processes—each completely different from the others—I saw the perfection in each of their individual stories as they unfolded, as well as in the bigger story of Zoe's adoption. Everything had to happen exactly as it did, in divine time, for Zoe and me to be united.

And such perfection! Could the trajectory of such events be anything else but proof that everything that happened was part of some larger divine plan and that our lives were all interconnected? I believed that what transpired was the highest triumph of the human spirit; it was like a tapestry whose splendor couldn't exist without all those ugly little knots and loose ends hidden on the underside.

I saw that love can take on many guises, I learned about the fruitlessness of assigning blame, and I realized that what may seem horrible up close is beautiful from a distance. I was reminded, once again, that life isn't about being perfect or not making mistakes; it is, I think, partly about doing what you believe is right, no matter how difficult.

I also realized that all those years I had struggled to accept that I was deaf and then went on to help other deaf people—especially deaf children—accept it for themselves, too, I hadn't only been doing it for me but had also been doing it for Zoe.

From the very moment I learned that Zoe existed, I knew that she and I were destined to be together. But after examining everyone's stories and digging into my own, I finally understood why—and why I had yearned for a daughter for all those years. It was as if the effect had come before the cause: I needed a daughter to better show me who I was, while showing me why I had needed her all along. I realized that I didn't need just a daughter—but a *deaf* daughter. I needed Zoe. I saw how all of my decisions and experiences—the schools I'd chosen to attend, friends I'd kept, boyfriends I'd left, and pageants I'd entered—had been grooming me to be Zoe's mother, allowing Zoe to become the confident young girl she is today.

The gifts *I* have received from Zoe being deaf truly began to dawn on me.

At first, this revelation presented a huge problem. I had no desire to put myself or my life out there, or make my journey and deep inner struggle to accept myself as a deaf person an open book for the entire world to read. I'd spent the first third of my life denying that struggle and finally accepted the fact that I'd struggled and made peace with it. But sharing it in a book was something entirely different.

Feeling very raw and naked, I labored to write these pages. I didn't want to expose myself or my vulnerabilities (to the Deaf community, in particular). I was afraid that many people would read it and not like some of the things I had to say. I was afraid of upsetting or offending members of my community whom I may not even know—and, even more, the friends and colleagues I care about. And it would tear me up inside to upset my mother. However, as I trusted my process, I felt myself opening up to and claiming myself as a deaf person even more deeply and powerfully than I knew was possible. With that came a new level of self-acceptance, so I took a leap of faith that those who loved me would understand.

In the end, I believe that healing happened not only for me but also for everyone else in our story—before a single word was even put down on the page. For example, after not seeing each other for five years, Jess and BJ, after being interviewed, met and reconciled their differences. Jess asked BJ why he had taken her to court, and he explained that he wanted to parent Celine and that it was the only way he felt that his voice would finally be heard, which Jess completely understood.

Jess felt awful about how she had treated BJ all through-out her pregnancy and after Celine was born and for not better understanding his point of view. Yet, she also real-ized how young she had been and how desperately she needed her parent's help. She was so grateful to her father and said that if it hadn't been for his undying support, she'd probably be taking care of Celine today, and not have graduated college, married, and made such a fulfilling life for herself. Looking back, she treasured the tough times most of all.

"Zoe taught me so much," she said. "Everything was for her. If I had a decision to make, I stepped back and said, 'OK, what's the best scenario?' Before, I just did what I wanted. She made me grow up and realize that life isn't just about yourself, and that you need to make sacrifices when you really love somebody."

BJ discovered that he was a lot stronger having had something to fight for—his child—and also that he had the willpower to stick with something that he truly believed in. Before his experiences with Zoe, BJ had a hard time dedicating himself to one thing and just staying with it. But after fighting for Zoe and loving her enough to let her go, he discovered just how much he loved working in the construction field and found the willpower to stay committed. "Zoe helped me to find out who I really am," he said. "Wherever I go, people will know her story."

Sandy and Stephane had been so upset when they discovered that Jess hadn't told them the whole truth about Celine's hearing, and who could blame them? But during an interview for this book, Stephane acknowledged, "A seventeen-year-old-girl got scared and brushed it under the rug. We've all done that—broken something and then replaced it before anybody knows. I'm not judging. You never know what somebody might do in the same situation."

Sandy, too, had her own realizations. "God had chosen us to take care of Celine because I had the connections," she said. "That was our purpose. We were her stepping-stone." Becoming all choked up she continued, "Celine was my butterfly—bound in a chrysalis and forming inside me. I protected her and gave her what she needed to grow. But I just couldn't protect her any longer. I had to open my arms and let her go."

Thank goodness Sandy passed Zoe's baby calendar on to Lois. That gem was ultimately passed down to me and was an important resource used in writing this book. Lois, while never once doubting her decision to adopt Mark, realized even more clearly how being with Celine had reaffirmed that decision, revealing a wondrous flow and order to everything that had happened in their lives.

* * *

IRONICALLY, it wasn't until a few weeks after we had brought Zoe home—when a good friend of mine said how wonderful it was that she was deaf—that it actually hit me that I had a *deaf* daughter. Oh, I knew that Zoe was deaf, but for so long I'd been so obsessed with getting her and so afraid of losing her that her being deaf hadn't really registered. Those first few weeks, I felt as if she had come to me with the world stacked against her. Ours was the *fifth* home in which she had lived in only eight short months—*the fifth home*—and even though it had all worked out perfectly, part of me felt hurt and angry that she had been rejected so many times. A fierce determination welled up inside me to prove to them—to prove to the world—that my daughter was going to be a lot more than just okay; she was going to take the world by storm.

But the biggest shock was back when Zoe turned two and then three years old. She was the *spitting image* of the girl Tim had described in his story—blonde and sassy, a little princess who carried herself and signed with such amazing confidence. It was as if he had seen into the future.

The ending of the adoption story was really just the beginning for Zoe and me, our family, and the others. At the time of this writing, with Zoe at ten years old, the lives of our cast of characters have twisted, turned, and evolved further.

Where are we all now, and how did we get there?

BJ

On February 1st, 2005, a thick, brown envelope came in the mail for BJ from New Horizons. Zoe had been home with us for almost three months and was content as could be and making great progress with her physical therapy. I had taken an eight-week leave from work to be with her, and we were together all the time. Christmas had come and gone, and we were all settling in.

BJ knew the envelope was coming because a couple days earlier New Horizons had sent a letter saying that they would be forwarding something. A whole stack of mail lay on the kitchen counter, and BJ went over to open it. His parents came over and stood by him as he pulled several letters out of the envelope, along with some photographs that fell to the floor. The three of them picked up the photos and started looking at them.

"Who are these people?" BJ said, seeming confused.

"Yeah, there are three boys here," his mother added. "I thought that she had only one brother."

"Well, maybe they're cousins," his father chimed in.

BJ quickly took one of the letters and started reading it, and his parents each took a letter to read as well.

Then his mother cried out, "Brandi? That's not the mother's name! Who's Brandi?"

BJ just couldn't believe it. "Wait a minute," he said, now looking at one of the photographs, "this isn't the family that she was with. She's got another family!"

He felt sick. They all felt sick and couldn't believe that no one had told them what had happened.

As BJ read my letter, his hands were shaking. I had sent three letters to the adoption agency a few months before for them to forward to him, but for some reason, they hadn't forwarded them until now. In the first letter, dated December 13th, I introduced myself and let him know that we had adopted Zoe. I remember writing how much we had wanted her, and how grateful we were having her as our daughter. I wanted him to know that. I had also included some photographs. In one of them, Zoe was sitting in a swing giggling while Tim pushed her, and in another, she had just finished eating and had Oreos all over her face.

In the next letter, dated January 3rd, I thanked him and his parents for the stuffed animal and the adorable outfit they had sent Zoe for Christmas via New Horizons, and in the following one, dated January 8th, I sent our regards along with several new photographs of Zoe.

It was quite a lot to take in at one time. Not hearing from anyone for months, BJ had thought that no news was good news—that Celine was with Sandy and Stephane and doing fine. After seeing their portfolio back when he had visited Celine at New Horizons, BJ had a vision of where she was going and was so relieved that she would be with such a good family. When he and his family found out about her hearing loss and that Sandy was a speech pathologist, they all thought, "She works in a hospital with doctors, and she'll be so good for her."

After BJ finished reading my first letter, he sat down at the kitchen table and read the other two, along with a letter from Marlys explaining that his daughter had gone to a new family. For ten minutes, he just sat there, going back and forth between the letters and photographs and feeling really strange—though he was finding out a "bad thing," it didn't seem so bad. Seeing that we were deaf and how happy Zoe was and how well she was doing, he even started thinking that perhaps it was a good thing. Later that day, he was grateful that she was with us and not with a different family.

It was just such a shock. It had been so hard for him *not* to fight for Celine in the first place. Then he made a gut-wrenching decision to let her go, only to discover that things hadn't worked out. Had he known, he felt he would've stepped in and said, "This is it. She has a dad right here in Algona who wants her so badly."

For two years, BJ was profoundly disappointed in himself and carried around a deep regret for not fighting harder for his little girl. Finally, in October of 2006, when Zoe was two and I drove with her to Algona to meet them, he let go of that feeling.

Years later, he told me how nervous he had been that day and how he had really wanted to make a good impression on us. He and Zoe spent an entire hour alone together—just running around in the back yard and playing. I can only imagine how healing it must have been for him. He and his family were all such lovely people.

BJ Briggs and his family came to visit. Left to right:
BJ, Angie, Dale, Joann (holding Zoe), me, and Tim.

Before we left, BJ's father pulled me over to the side and said, "Brandi, I want you to know that you've just ended two years of heartache for BJ and our whole family. He no longer feels like he made a mistake."

After that, BJ arranged through New Horizons for us to be able to get together on our own. It worked out perfectly because whenever we traveled from Sioux Falls to Minnesota, I let them know and we would meet up. We also began emailing each other, and I'd send him pictures of Zoe that he'd hang all over his refrigerator. To this day, it is covered with her pictures.

"Zoe helped me to realize that if you're going to make a decision, then make it," BJ said, "and if it comes from

BJ AND ZOE

inside of you, and you feel that it's right, it's going to be pretty darn close to being right. The worst that can happen is that somebody will say that you're wrong."

As for Marlys, we may never know why she didn't tell BJ that Sandy and Stephane had relinquished Celine and that she had gone back to foster care. While I can certainly appreciate BJ's anguish, in a way I believe that what Marlys did turned out to be a blessing. It prevented him from fighting for Zoe all over again, saving him and his family so much extra pain and heartache. And it allowed Zoe to find where she really belonged.

In the winter of 2012, BJ applied for a license to start his own construction company and named it Zoe Construction. At the time of this writing, BJ is thirty-four, single, and living in Algona, Iowa, about ten miles from his parents. While his busy work schedule has prevented him from seeing Zoe over the past few years, his parents, who think of Zoe as their granddaughter, came to visit us last winter, and it was almost as if BJ were there himself. His love for Zoe fills me with such joy every single day.

SANDY AND STEPHANE

About a month before Sandy and Stephane had visited Zoe and me in April of 2005, they received a phone call from Marlys one evening, "There is a baby boy waiting for you. His parents have terminated their rights. It's done. There's no waiting time. Nothing is going to take this child away from you. And, by the way, you've got to find a name for him by tomorrow. We open our doors at 5:00 AM."

Shocked beyond words, they said, "We have a name for a girl but not a boy!" They spent the rest of the evening picking out a name for their new son and decided on Jacques. The next day when they met his birth parents and told them the name they had chosen, his birth parents started crying. "All of the men's names in our family start with the letter J," they said. And that was that.

Thinking about it all, Stephane said, "You could say that God was watching over us, but it was through Marlys. She did it that way on purpose, knowing that we couldn't go through another adoption ordeal."

Jacques has red hair, looks Irish, and is feisty like you won't believe! He brings out the humor in everyone, and his teachers say that he is so funny he should be in television commercials. In 2006, their family moved from Sioux Falls, South Dakota, to Toronto, Canada, and then Stephane took a new job in Boulder, Colorado, in 2011, which entails a lot less travel. Sandy was very happy about that. She still works as a speech pathologist. Antoine is eleven years old, and Jacques is eight.

JESS

After we brought Zoe home, I felt compelled to call New Horizons, asking them to find out if Jess wanted to see Zoe again. I realized that I had been so obsessed with adopting Zoe that I never even stopped to think about how Jess must have felt after all that she had been through, relinquishing her not once but *three* times. I wanted her to know that Zoe was really fine. She's growing, thriving, and communicating. I wanted her to see that while we were embracing the fact that she was deaf, we would not let it define her.

Jess said yes, so Zoe and I drove to Blue Earth, Minnesota, and visited her (and Lois, as well). I brought along some of Zoe's books; one of them was about farm animals, her favorite. She read it to Jess, signing the names of all the animals.

I remember sitting in New Horizons that day. Zoe, who was a little over a year old, was standing in her white pants and pink shirt, holding onto the couch. When Jess came into the room and saw her, she immediately leaped toward her, as if her mother's instincts had taken over, but then she caught herself, realizing that Zoe didn't know her. It was such a natural reaction, and my heart so went out to her. Appreciating her enthusiasm and wanting to honor her visit with Zoe, I went to buy some milk for Zoe's sippy cup, giving them some time alone together.

When I returned a half hour later, I watched the two of them through a two-way mirror so they couldn't see me. Zoe was sitting on Jess's lap and playing with her hair. When I finally walked into the room and Zoe saw me, Jess set her down and she ran straight to me, signing, "Mommy, Mommy."

I'd always known that Jess had given me an angel, but now I could see how much she loved Zoe and decided that she would always be a part of her life. Also, I didn't want Zoe to ever wonder about her birth mother. Jess and I began emailing, and over the following year or so, while she was in college, we all saw each other two more times. We met for dinner and went to her dorm room, which was filled with pictures of Zoe all over the walls.

It's funny. I remember people asking me back then if I was afraid that Jess would want to take Zoe back, and I always said no, that I knew that *I* was her mother. The fear in peoples' minds came from all the negative media hype—of cases years ago where the judge gave back a baby to the birth parents. That doesn't happen anymore.

After some time had passed, Jess emailed me, saying that now that Zoe was getting older it was becoming too difficult for her to keep seeing her. It was because she needed to take a break from all the memories and live the college life. She had to find herself again. I understood all too well. Yet, I wanted her to always know where to find us, in case she ever needed to reach out to Zoe, and continued sending her pictures and updates every now and then. In the summer of 2007, when Tim got a promotion at work and we had to relocate to Clearwater, Florida, I let Jess know, just in case she wanted to see Zoe, since it had been a year. She did; so Zoe, Blake, and I went to her father's house (he had invited his entire family), and we spent the whole day there, having lunch and planting flowers, with her father videotaping the whole thing. Jess cried and cried when we left. We didn't see her again until three years later in March of 2010, when she visited us in Clearwater on Zoe's sixth birthday.

What a day.

Way before Zoe could comprehend it, I had been telling her this adoption story. I didn't want there to be a day when I finally "told her"—I wanted her to always know. As a four- and five-year-old, she would tell me that she was in Jess's tummy and was born and then Jess gave her to me. But now, as a fully grown child, I had no idea how she would react to actually seeing Jess and spending the entire day with her. You teach your children what you feel is important, hoping that when they're older they'll embrace it.

But to see it all come to fruition in one day was overwhelming! I was so proud of Zoe.

I took Jess to her classroom, and as soon as Zoe saw her, she ran right over and hugged her leg. Jess knelt down and hugged her back and then started crying, of course, as did

I. Later in the day, she signed to Jess, "You gave birth to me." She understood that Jess was her birth mother who gave her life, that I was the mother who was raising her, and that we both loved her very much. At one point, she put her arms around both of us and squeezed us tight, as if to say that she understood.

It felt so great to see my influence on her, especially concerning something of this magnitude. What a deep thing for a six-year-old to understand, I thought. It just confirmed for me what I had always known—and wanted Zoe to know—that there is enough love to go around for all of us.

I realize that having an open adoption of this kind may not be right for other adoptive families, but it is right for ours. When I see Zoe embracing who she is and where she came from in such a beautiful way, I see my own self in her and know even more that she is truly my daughter.

When it came time for Jess to leave, Zoe said, "So long. See you again sometime."

We received Jess's wedding invitation in the summer of 2012, when Zoe was eight, and the following September she and I flew up to Blue Earth, Minnesota, where the wedding was taking place. Zoe was a junior bridesmaid. At the time, I didn't even know if Jess had realized that it was Zoe who had taught her how to really love someone, but she had. Lois was invited, too.

Zoe looked darling in her waterfall blue dress that highlighted her golden hair, as she stood with all of the grown-up bridesmaids enveloped in their sea of blue. I had already explained to her that Jess had fallen in love and that she wanted Zoe to be part of the wedding because Jess loved her. Yet, as Zoe walked down the aisle all alone, her air of confidence so palpable I could practically reach out and touch it, I wondered what she was thinking.

She took her place at the altar with the others and watched quietly as Jess walked down the aisle, a vision of beauty herself draped in white, and then she waited patiently as Jess and her groom, Jerrick, turned and faced the pastor. When he began speaking, Zoe looked to Ann Marie whom we had brought along as her interpreter, so that she could understand.

"Jessica Lynn," the interpreter signed, "do you take Jerrick Lee to be your lawful, wedded husband, for richer or for poorer, in sickness and in health, till death do you part?"

"I do," Jess said.

"Then with the power vested in me, I now pronounce you husband and wife."

After their kiss, the organ pronouncing their way, Jess, before retracing her steps, went over to Zoe, crouched down in front of her and gave her a big hug and then said, "I love you."

For me, that hug contained all the love that had brought Zoe to that wonderful place and would surround her in the future. In the winter of 2014, Jess gave birth to a daughter, whom she named Adelynne Zoe. I don't know when and where we will all see each other again, but I know we will.

ZOE AND JESS AT JESS'S WEDDING

THE RARUS'S—BRANDI, TIM, ZOE, BLAKE, CHASE, AND AUSTIN

It just amazes me how many people tell me that Zoe looks just like me. (These days, we even have our hair cut the same way.) When I explain that we adopted her, they are shocked and say, "But she looks *so much* like you," to which I respond, "I know. But it wasn't my doing, it was God's."

Zoe wants to be like me, and I do my best every day to teach her by example. She sees the way I am in the world, that I am comfortable with both hearing and deaf people.

She knows my opinions about things and how Tim and I are both proud of who we are and of our community. She knows that we embrace our Deaf Culture, yet are in no way limited by it. Already, she is so much more comfortable in her own skin than I was at her age.

A few years ago, when she was six, Zoe and my then-ten-year-old son, Chase, and I were in my bedroom. Chase and I were sitting on the bed talking. Wanting to be included in our conversation, she kept signing, "What are you saying?" but I kept ignoring her because I was totally engrossed in my conversation with Chase. Finally, after about two minutes, she looked at me hard and signed, "Stop talking and sign!" as fiercely as if she were saying, "Hey, don't ignore me!"

Initially, I felt awful, thinking that I, of all people—who knows exactly what it feels like to be excluded—had left her out of the conversation. But then I thought, *You go, girl!* I felt so proud of her because there she was at six years old, already standing up for herself in a way I never had.

In the summer of 2011, our family moved from Clearwater back to Austin, Texas, so that Zoe could attend the Texas School for the Deaf (TSD). Just as Camp Mark Seven was an eye-opener for me, TSD was the same for Zoe. Even though she has deaf parents and complete communication at home, she was mainstreamed in Clearwater, so her interaction with deaf adults was limited. However, at TSD, she has deaf teachers and is in an environment that embraces ASL. She has really become Tim's daughter since attending the school, as she takes great pride in being deaf and in our culture and language. She just loves it there, and

Tim and I are so grateful for their program and educators who are so committed to giving deaf children a great education. Zoe plays volleyball and basketball on deaf teams. Her language is continuing to blossom, and we are very proud of her. As of this writing, Zoe is in her third year at TSD and is in the fourth grade. Of course, she is thriving, like I always knew she would. One of her best friends is Skylar, Ann Marie's adopted daughter from China. They are like two peas in a pod. Skylar is hearing but signs, of course; when need be, she is Zoe's little interpreter.

ZOE AND SKYLAR

Blake is a sophomore in high school, Chase is in eighth grade, and Austin is in sixth. With the city of Austin so deaf friendly and people signing out in the open in most public places, the boys are signing so much better and have a good mix of hearing and deaf friends. They are part of a large Kids of Deaf Adults (KODA) community, and the friends they meet at school and bring home have all taken an interest in learning sign language.

The boys adore their sister and really watch out for her. Zoe holds her own with them and is right out there with them playing basketball, football, or baseball. She is incredibly outgoing—very much our social butterfly, to use Lois's description of her as an infant. Our lives are in balance.

Tim is succeeding in his eighth year as vice president of sales at ZVRS, a company that was spun off from Communication Service for the Deaf (CSD). We were so grateful that Tim's boss allowed Tim to relocate to Austin, so that Zoe could attend the Texas School for the Deaf (TSD).

As the Director of Business Development for CSD, I provide communication solutions for our many customers. These are companies large and small, both nonprofits and Fortune 500 companies that have deaf and hard-of-hearing employees. I believe Austin will be our home for a very long time.

I would like to note that with the closing of so many Deaf Schools around the country these days due to budget cuts, many deaf children are not as fortunate as Zoe and are unable to attend schools such as TSD. The NAD is putting its efforts toward promoting the continuation and strengthening of our Deaf Schools, which is mandated by law.

MILESTONES

In 2008, CSD sold the video portion of the company and launched the new brand name for its products and services—ZVRS—named after Zoe! We are proud! It happened like this. One evening, several of Tim's colleagues were over for dinner, and I introduced them to Zoe and told them her adoption story. Well, the vice president of marketing was really touched by the story, and the following day, he proposed using the letter "Z" in honor of Zoe, as the company's logo. They use it as a symbol for deaf people all across America embracing the good life and to encourage deaf children to be whomever they want to be.

I remember thinking how awesome it was that before this book was even published, her story was being told. In fact, a video of Tim, Zoe, and me is on the company's website, and there's even a picture of Jess and her parents with Zoe on placement day.

At ten years old, Zoe is a shining light for deaf children growing up in America today—loving herself, her life, and the fact that she is deaf. And that she came to Tim and me through adoption and not through pregnancy makes the whole experience that much more meaningful.

ACKNOWLEDGMENTS

Brandi

Jess Urban: You have given us the most incredible, amazing gift. There are no words I can use to express my gratitude for your choosing Tim and me to be Zoe's parents. As promised, she will always know you, and as she grows older, I'm sure that she will be grateful for the choices you made out of love for her.

BJ Briggs: Thank you for stepping aside and allowing Zoe to be placed for adoption. We know how much you wanted to raise her. One day, I'm sure that she will come to understand the sacrifice you made.

Bryan Simmering and Sonja Trelstad: You both were the hands that guided Jess through those nine months of pregnancy, helping her to make the tough decision of choosing adoption, knowing that Zoe was your first grandchild. Thank you for that unconditional love.

Dale and Joann Briggs: Thank you for being so welcoming to my family, for the effort you make to remain a part of Zoe's life. You are the kind of parents to BJ that I hope I am and always will be to Zoe.

Stephane and Sandy Billat: Thank you for being so open to this story being written and for how you loved Zoe. Your difficult choice to relinquish her was what finally brought her home.

Lois and Chuck Strack: We could not have asked for better foster parents! You have been a blessing to so many families and so many children—but especially to Zoe!

Sean Bellanger: Thank you for making Zoe a part of the Z family, and for allowing us to relocate so that she could attend TSD. We are beyond grateful.

Glenn Yeffeth: Our publisher at BenBella Books, thanks for agreeing that *Finding Zoe* was a story worth telling. Thank You! And thanks to the entire BenBella team.

Rita Barry Corke: A publicist worth millions, thanks for taking on our project with such passion; your wisdom throughout this process has been a guiding light.

To my girlfriends, who have always walked beside me, celebrated my victories, and caught me each time I fell:

Kelly Lange: For being the most positive and accepting of friends. Your nonjudgment of others is a quality I have long admired. Thank you for your graphic work and creativity toward my brand.

Melody Stein: For your love, loyalty, and support and for being such an inspiration. Pizza soon at Mozzeria!

Lisa Dyas: For 40 years of friendship and a lifetime of memories. What fun we had growing up together. I so admire the strong woman you have become.

Ann Marie Mickelson: For being a loving friend, sister, and sounding board—and always an advocate for Zoe. I am as thankful for Zoe's friendship with Skylar as I am for ours!

Sheila McFarland: Thank you, She, for being my calm in the middle of the storm right before I brought Zoe home. Your support for her, as well as the love I know you have for my sons, is a treasure. It is you who taught me what it means to be a mother of boys.

Naomi McCown: Our gourmet chef turned sign language interpreter! Thank you for being my ears and voice at some of the most significant moments of my life, for the birth of my sons and now for my journey with *Finding Zoe*. Love you so!

Dr. Patty Hughes, CEO of GLAD (Greater Los Angeles Agency on Deafness): For showing me what a strong Deaf woman can be. I learned so much from your example and wisdom. Thank you for your edits and feedback of this book and for ensuring that all the facts represent our Deaf community with the grace it deserves.

Alex Long: For your edits of "Deaf" and "deaf" . . . whew!

David Rosenbaum: Thank you for being someone I could completely trust to do right by me, for your objectivity, and for your knowledge and understanding of our community.

Nancy Rarus: You were a wealth of information and a resource for so much of our Deaf History. Gramps would be proud. Thank you for your contributions and research.

John Nelson: What can I say? You were a gift to Gail and me, your wisdom our guide to this story unfolding the way it was meant to. Thank you for taking this on, for believing in it, and for your connections in the publishing world.

The folks at Communication Service for the Deaf (CSD): You have been a part of my life for the past twenty years. Ben Soukup: Your support for my "adoption leave" when I first brought Zoe home is still very much appreciated. Chris Soukup: Your flexibility with my work status and schedule so that I could write this book—thank you! I am extremely grateful for the support of the company and for our mission.

Gail Harris: Thank you for taking this project on with such passion and giving it life. This book may be about me, but it is just as much your story. You befriended everyone involved along the way and created a safe place for healing. Thank you for reaffirming our belief that by doing what is right for ourselves, we also do what is right for others. Thank you for sharing my journey of self-acceptance with me and for writing this story, so that Zoe will always know how much she is loved. I know I speak for everyone involved when I say, "Thank you from the bottom of our hearts. Thank you!"

My mother, Ann Falk: Thank you for always having my back, supporting me through thick and thin, and being my greatest cheerleader. I love you!

To my dad, Bill Sculthorpe: Whom I have come to know and appreciate as an adult much more than I did as a child. I am so much like you. I love you.

A very special thanks to my Home Team in Austin, Texas.

The Kids—Blake, Chase, Austin, and Zoe: You guys rock! Dad and I want nothing but the very best for you. Go after your dreams.

Tim: You have been an incredible husband and the most amazing father. Thank you for encouraging me to go after my dreams, for your love and support. When I look at Zoe today, she is so your daughter! We are so fortunate to have our family. Thank you from the bottom of my heart for all you do and who you are.

Gail

First and foremost I want to thank Brandi Rarus for living such an amazing life and for being such an extraordinary person. Wherever I turned as a writer, jewels and riches abounded. Her openness to dig deep into murky territory, where she had not originally intended to go, lest the entire world go with her, humbles me to the core. How wonderful it is to see her take her rightful place in the world and to be a part of making that happen. This was truly a symbiotic partnership, based on the shared belief that life's perfection is there for us to capture it, that we must capture it in order to fully live, and that if we don't, it is truly a shame. I also want to thank Tim Rarus for taking me back with him to that critical time and place in his life and inviting me in— as a student leader at Gallaudet University in 1988 (not that he needed much prodding). What a gift! Tim's passionate expression using ASL has touched me deeply, and I hope someday to converse with him in his language. Not knowing a single deaf person before working with Brandi and Tim, I found my mind and soul being filled in such brand new ways. Thank you both for introducing me to a world that I never knew existed, yet isn't at all separate from my own.

I want to thank Jess Urban, Zoe's birth mother; BJ Briggs, Zoe's birth father; and Sandy and Stephane Billet, Zoe's first adoptive parents, for opening up to me about one of the most difficult times in their lives. The questions I asked them weren't easy, but each gracefully shared their experiences, so that this marvelous story could be told. Their love for Zoe and commitment to follow their own truths, no matter how difficult, is the stuff that great lives (and stories) are made of. To Lois and Chuck Strack, Zoe's foster parents, thank your for sharing your story about your son, Mark; for facilitating some of the back and forths between myself and Sandy and Stephane; and especially for your wisdom, Lois.

I'd also like to thank Sonia Trelstad, Bryan Simmering, Joann and Dale Briggs, Angie Garman, Ann Falk, Nancy Rarus, Ann Marie Mickelson, and Sheila McFarland for helping me to better understand what really happened and to better understand Brandi.

I could not have written this book without devouring Oliver Sack's *Seeing Voices: A Journey into the World of the Deaf*. Most of the facts about Deaf History and Deaf Culture and the Gallaudet Uprising—a good portion of Chapter 3—were taken from what is written there, including his unique perceptions of thought and language as they relate to the deaf. He was the hearing person who really turned me on to Deaf Culture. Other historical facts were taken from *Far from the Tree* by Andrew Solomon, and additional information about the Gallaudet Protest, not including Tim's personal experiences, were taken from *The Week the World Heard Gallaudet* by Jack Gannon. To all three authors, a profound thank you.

Kudos to Becky Koivisto, transcriber *spectaculaire*, who, for almost two years worked at lightning speed, while sharing with me the profundity of what I had uncovered and validating my hunch that I was truly on to something.

My deepest, deepest thanks go to John Nelson, our premiere genius-of-an-editor and guy with the hugest heart, who helped me to weave together all of the pieces of the story and to trust my instincts. Without him, this book simply would not have happened. Mahalo, John. And to Elisabeth Rinaldi, also the editor of my dreams, who then helped to spin all the hard work we had already accomplished into gold.

A big thank you to my dear friend and editor, Natalie Reid, who helped to edit the prologue in the early stages, and who never lets me settle for writing anything less than the best; to Cynthia Mitchell and Julie McNamee, our copyeditors; and to Barbara Deal and Hal Bennett for their trusted guidance regarding publishing.

I want to thank all of the folks at BenBella Books: to Glenn Yeffeth, our publisher, who fell in love with this story and had to publish it; to Erin Kelley, our editor, and the rest of the BenBella staff with whom I have had the privilege of working. And my sincerest appreciation to Rita

Barry Corke, our publicist, for hanging in there with us through thick and thin and giving us her all.

To my friend Margaret Nies, who keeps me sane like no one in the world, and George Jaidar, whose wise teachings allowed me to see the perfection in this story and helps me strive to see it in all stories, especially my own. For that, I am and always will be eternally grateful.

Finally, to Bill and Lucas, who supported me at the dinner table and everywhere else for the past five years while I worked on this project, and listened to me talk about practically nothing else, I thank you with all my heart.

* * *

WE, BRANDI AND GAIL, would also like to thank Robert Sculthorpe and Rich Panico and the folks at Integrated Project Management, Inc. for their generous donations to our Kickstarter.com campaign. It is because of you that our awesome publicity team has been able to get to work.

ABOUT THE AUTHORS

Brandi Rarus

Deaf since age six after contracting spinal meningitis, Brandi Rarus could speak and read lips but felt caught between the Deaf World and hearing world—fitting into neither. Growing up in the 70s and 80s, when being deaf was still considered a handicap and prejudice was pervasive, Brandi faced great personal struggle. It wasn't until she reached a turning point, finally realizing you don't need to hear to live a fulfilled life, that she became empowered with a newfound spirit and was chosen as Miss Deaf America. From signing the National Anthem at a Chicago Cubs game to speaking at corporate conferences, Brandi traveled the country speaking out for deaf children and building awareness of what it means to be deaf.

But that's not the whole story . . . her dream of becoming a mother was realized when she met and married Tim Rarus, an advocate for deaf people whose work inspired the landmark Americans with Disabilities Act. Together they have paved the way to bring about new technologies that promote equal access in communication. Brandi and Tim live in Austin, Texas, with their four children: three hearing boys and the youngest, Zoe, a deaf girl whom they adopted and who needed to find parents uniquely prepared to help her thrive in a silent world. Today, Brandi and her family are tirelessly dedicated to ensuring that all children like Zoe find their rightful place in our world by shedding light on both the adoption process and the necessity for early intervention with children of different needs.

Gail Harris

Award-winning writer and teacher of the intuitive process, Gail Harris has also experienced the joy of having adopted a child. She brings her knowledge of the adoption process and in vitro fertilization to this book, along with her ability to articulate from a hearing person's perspective all that is fascinating about the Deaf experience. In the four years that it took to write *Finding Zoe*, Gail conducted more than seventy-five interviews to uncover, as only she could, the beautiful yet sometimes excruciatingly painful stories behind adoption. Gail is the author of *Your Heart Knows the Answer* and a featured blogger on several popular parenting blogs. She lives with her husband and son in Framingham, Massachusetts.

RESOURCES

THIS BOOK IS about many things. It is about being deaf, Deaf Culture, and Deaf History. It is about having an unintended pregnancy. It is about adoption and good parenting. It is about making the right choices, no matter how difficult they may be. It is about fulfilling your destiny. It is about coming home to self and family.

There are many resources that we'd like to share with our readers: for those of us who are on a journey of self-discovery; for moms, pregnant teens, or anyone else who is dealing with an unintended pregnancy; for people who are interested in or have been touched by adoption; and for deaf people and hearing people who are connected with the Deaf community or are interested in learning about Deaf Culture and ASL. To keep our information up to date, we have placed this information on our websites. Please visit us at brandirarus.com and gailharrisauthor.com.